SMART LEADERSHIP

By Anthony S. Vlamis

AMA Management Briefing

AMA Publications Division
American Management Association

For information on how to order additional
copies of this publication, see page 71.

Contents

Acknowledgments

My sincerest thanks to Dan R. Bannister, James Champy, Jim Doyle, Mortimer R. Feinberg, Jack H. Grossman, Frances Hesselbein, Thomas R. Horton, Victor Kiam, Ed Ridolfi, and Glen Tobe, who gave so generously of their time to make this briefing possible. To Amy Zuckerman whose irrepressible enthusiasm persuaded me to take on the project and to Lydia Long and Jim Gerard for their professional help with the interviews. To Richard Lally, my special thanks, to Geoffrey Steck for his insightful commentary, and to Florence Stone, my house editor on this project for her patience and always constructive ideas.

To my family, for their love and encouragement

Preface

Leadership is a perennial topic among business readers; it has been the subject of many fine books. This briefing adds a quick reading and positive take on the subject. It targets issues that executives and managers have asked about. As Peter Senge observed in an article in *Organizational Dynamics*, leadership has been, and continues to be, the most popular topic of discussion within organizations because it is always evolving and constantly changing.

From the dawn of the Industrial Revolution through the early 1980s, the protocols and ideas about leadership evolved pretty much in a straightforward fashion and were fairly static. But recently many of the tenets of leadership have changed. And with cause. The emergence of the global economy, fast-paced changes in technology, and shifts in structure, strategy, and culture are all factors.

Most business leaders recognize that there have been changes, and they have good reason to wonder:

- What crisis will hit next?

- How can they keep up with, let alone process, the continual barrage of information--about their industry, functional skills, customer needs, competitors, overseas markets, technology and the economy?

- Where can they find enough skilled workers?

- How can they navigate through ever-changing regulations and the constant threat of lawsuits?

Clearly, we see unprecedented change within and outside organizations. It's a good bet such change will continue and, in fact, will accelerate. So how can leaders learn to effectively and artfully prepare for the next millennium?

To help answer these question, in the face of myriad future uncertainties, we asked a select team of business executives, trainers, consultants, authors, and academics for their thoughts about these concerns and the following 11 questions:

1. Do you have a personal vision of good leadership in these times?

2. What do you see as the five or so defining characteristics of good leaders and managers?

3. How does a leader get people to follow?

4. How does a leader inspire leadership at every level of the organization?

5. How does a leader develop a team culture in an organization?

6. How do you attract the best people?

7. What are the main challenges/issues today's leaders face?

8. How does a leader/manager cope with the seemingly endless barage of information flow?

9. How do you deal with burnout, on a personal level and among those on whom you count most?

10. Who among current leaders or managers would you consider to be a model in the current fast-changing environment?

11. Will tomorrow's leaders be different from our stereotype of today's top executives? If so, how so?

Not surprisingly, there was quite a bit of agreement around topics like the qualities of leaders. In other areas, there was diverse and sometimes contrasting opinion. For example, Ed Ridolfi makes a clear distinction between a leader and a manager, arguing that the leaders are those with vision and purpose, and likely to be mavericks, whereas managers are the ones who execute the strategy of the leader. Some feel that leadership can be learned,

and others like James Champy feel there are certain innate leadership qualities that can be sharpened but not necessarily learned. In a time when the
social compact between workers and management seems dissolved, there is
a refreshingly consistent and clear voice of agreement over how important
people are, how connected the leader must be (see Glen Tobe) and how to
address the needs of young people moving up in today's organization (see
Dan Bannister).

This book will provide you with a concise list of the benchmarks and practices of great leaders and great companies and perhaps help you leverage
more of the talents hidden within yourself and your organization.

—Anthony S. Vlamis

Chapter 1

DAN R. BANNISTER

Leadership Summary

Dan R. Bannister worked his way up from an electronics technician at Dyncorp in 1953 to president and CEO in 1985 and chairman in 1997 of this $1.5 billion high-tech company based in Reston, Virginia. With 45 years at the same company under his belt, Bannister may be among the last of the breed of one-company managers. But he embraces and manages change as nimbly as any up-and-coming, self-respecting company- and career-hopping executive today. Under his leadership, Dyncorp has reinvented everything from its structure (from NYSE-traded company to Employee Stock Ownership Plan) to the industry it serves (from airline and aircraft maintenance services to information technology and management solutions).

■ DO YOU HAVE A PERSONAL VISION OF GOOD LEADERSHIP IN THESE TIMES?

The main requirements of leadership have changed dramatically over the last several years. The main difference is in people relations. The working environment and the culture of the company are of much more concern to a CEO today than they were in the past. Ten years ago we didn't have to deal with things like equal employment opportunity or on-the-job harassment, sexual or otherwise. Not that we shouldn't have, but in today's working environment, the culture you create demands more of your time and attention than it did in the past.

A leader must set examples, goals, inspire people, motivate, help

1

establish objectives and strategic plans. I have always stressed being a change agent. When I think about Jack Welch's reign since 1981, I think that what he's done with that company is to change it. He preaches change and he's known as a change agent. He sold off 17 companies and he has grown that business; helped GE become the most admired corporation in America, if not in the world. The leadership he provides is an essential ingredient to his success.

He told everyone that GE was going to be number one or number two in any business they're in. That kind of vision and leadership galvanized everybody in the company. Everyone knew, whatever business we're in, if we're not number one or two, we won't be in that business. It's very powerful.

Welch once said that if he had to pick three criteria that were most important for future leaders at GE, they would be: (1) they have to be comfortable in global situations, (2) they must have an endless supply of energy; and (3) they have know how to energize people.

I don't know whether being in one company my entire career helps or hinders my effectiveness as a leader. It may convey a sense of security to some people. When people have commented to me about my long tenure, they mostly have done so in a positive tone. I'm sure there are some people who don't feel the same way.

The only time you need to bring someone in from the outside is when the company is changing and it needs someone who has knowledge and skills in the areas in which the company is changing. This company came to a point where we were going to become an information technology services company, a field in which I didn't have particular expertise. If I were 20 years younger it wouldn't have bothered me at all, but at the age I was at when I became CEO, it was clear I was not going to carry the company forward the next 10 years. It wouldn't make sense for me to become sufficiently skilled in the new technology to lead the company. That's why we went outside the company to find someone who did have experience and competency to carry us into those new markets.

I've led the company into new markets before.

I went and learned about an industry we were going into, such as commercial aviation services and specialty contracting. I read, got involved in the industry, learned the players, did market studies—standard stuff. The difference between now and then is—the primary driver for bringing in a replacement for me last year—had to do more with my age than with my ability. We have changed this company from what it was to one of the largest information technology companies in the U.S. To keep driving the company into the information technology service business requires a leader who has a five- to ten-year horizon. I don't have and didn't want to have that, not as the CEO.

■ WHAT DO YOU SEE AS THE DEFINING CHARACTERISTICS OF GOOD LEADERS AND MANAGERS?

BREADTH OF KNOWLEDGE AND LONG-TERM PERFORMANCE

It's the breadth of what you know that counts, not the path you took. You used to be able to count the rungs of the corporate ladder to the top, and you could see what you had to do to get to each one. Nowadays, it doesn't matter your discipline. Rather, it is how you distinguish yourself through your performance.

If you're the CFO of a company, for instance, you have to demonstrate you are more than the manager of finances—you have to demonstrate you can lead people, understand the basic business, handle marketing and customer relations. Without those skills you can't be CEO. Not all CFOs can or want to do that. You can be the most distinguished CFO in an industry, but that doesn't qualify you or give you a shot at being CEO of a business.

CONTINUAL LEARNING

Continue developing your own skills. A leader's most important skill today is technology, technology, technology. If you're not computer literate, if you're not able to figure out how to manage information today effectively, you're probably not going to be a good leader. It's another major difference between now and the past. Instant communications today expedite decision making and analysis, and at the same time open the door for a huge increase in communications.

PEOPLE SKILLS

You have to focus on people because building a strong team of managers and employees is very critical. It relates to the shortage of workers. Employees today have multiple choices for opportunities; it wasn't that way 10 years ago. So you have to focus on creating a dynamic work environment to keep employee retention up.

STUDYING WHAT LEADERS OF OTHER COMPANIES DO

You can't pick this up on your own. In 1982, before I became president here,

I went through the Harvard Executive Management program. That taught me one important thing: There is no one and only right answer. As we studied three to five case studies a day, I came to appreciate that there are always two or three possible approaches to any challenge or problem. Figuring out the best one for your company at any particular time is the CEO's job.

EARN TRUST

People's values are different today. Loyalty to a company, for the most part, doesn't exist as it did in the past. But that's okay because today you can still find plenty of loyalty. It's just different. Today loyalty is attached to a project or an objective.

An important element of building trust is building ownership. I don't mean stock ownership, though we have that, too. We want people to be accountable for what the company is doing and where it's going. To do that, we have to make them part of our strategic planning team. Having a piece of the plan helps assure they will buy into it. So commitment goes along with it. Instead of sitting on the bench watching the game, our people plan the plays, then help execute them. That's pretty exciting. We carry that all the way down the organizations—for instance, to our business units.

A WILLINGNESS TO TAKE RISKS

Early in my career, in 1955, I undertook what was then a huge high-risk military project, something the company had never done before, and I made it a success. The Air Force was putting in all new avionics in a certain airplane, taking apart and upgrading all the electrical and electronic wiring and instrumentation systems. No one had done it before except the company that did the prototype. I talked the customer into letting us do one. It was successful, and the company got a lot more business and raised itself to a higher plateau. I was in charge of the team that did that job. I think I wanted to do it because it was such a challenge, such an interesting project. I love that sort of stuff. It was fun to do.

Whenever I tell someone else what to do to shape their career, I say do something to be noticed, something that makes a difference in the company. It's how I worked my way up at Dyncorp. At first I was put in charge of a couple of small projects, and they were very successful. I took a couple of not-so-good customer situations and turned them around. I was just young and gutsy enough to try. It did not feel like that big a risk to me, like risking your company or risking an investment. There is no handbook on how to evaluate risk. A lot of it is intuitive. Very seldom has it failed, regarding people. You develop a sense when you're around long enough, when something feels right or doesn't. If it doesn't feel right, you had better not do it or you had better get some information first. That's what a leader does: provides an opportunity for managers, teams, and employees to give you all the facts concerning a situation that you need in order to evaluate and decide what the best course of action is. You have to sort out fact and fiction, or fact and opinion.

CREATE BUY-IN

We always give the management team veto rights on a deal. We don't sell that many units, but when we do, we always do that. After our company went private in 1988, I immediately sold off the electrical contracting business we had built from scratch into a $300 million enterprise. We brought a buyer into the picture and the management team rejected it. So we didn't do the deal. We sold it to someone else, someone they wanted. The smart companies do business this way.

It's a fatal mistake when a corporate office dictates what to do to those who have responsibility for business units.

■ WHAT ARE THE MAIN CHALLENGES/ISSUES TODAY'S LEADERS FACE?

HOW TO LAUNCH CHANGE

I may be from the old school of management as a one-company man, but I am not averse to change. I've implemented plenty of change. I work hard to prepare people and the organization for constant change.

It's important not just to react but to initiate change. We've changed the company at least 10 times. We've made major structural changes as well as changes to our business and our client base. It was different then. Change did not occur as rapidly. We did not have the technology tools we have today. Those technology tools are what's changing rapidly.

Our incentive program provides opportunities to motivate people to be change agents.

At the beginning of the year we sit down with employees and managers and agree on what their personal objectives are for the year and discuss change—what's going on, what will be different a year from now other than higher profits. What about the structure, people, clients, market, expansion? Those are all aspects of change. How are you going to get there, to create competitive advantage that you do not have now, because the competitive advantage you have now will be stale then? You have to assume your competitors are smart and are going to figure out a way to beat you. You won't win every single time, but you had better win most of the time. It's our management incentive plan.

Beyond that, effecting change is not just tied to financial rewards. You have to build an environment in which people understand that they are managing change. You do that in your communications. It's important to build a company that can be a little bold, a little radical at times. People must be encouraged to express new ideas, to look around them at what's going on in the world, not just their little world but the whole world.

TRACKING COMPETITORS AND INDUSTRY TRENDS

Five years ago, contractors did business with the U.S. government through the U.S. mail. Offices would be swimming in mounds and mounds of paper. Today it is becoming more and more electronic. Some agencies of government have said in a couple of years they will not be sending any more paper. If you don't know how to do business with the government through e-mail and the Internet, you won't do business with them. This is a radical change—it's almost unbelievable. That means there are lots of opportunities for managers to change their processes. If you have an executive who has his feet stuck in the mud, saying this e-commerce doesn't make sense, that business won't be around very long. In this case, the customer is changing the way we do business. I have to figure out how to get a competitive advantage out of it.

DOING BUSINESS ELECTRONICALLY

Doing business with the government electronically is just one small piece of electronic commerce. Doing business electronically also means the way you present your proposals and credentials is done electronically, and in person, which is a major change in marketing techniques. In the past, we wrote lengthy proposals, sometimes thousands of pages, sent them in boxes, and the government had people sitting around a table reading these volumes. Most government agencies have done away with that. Now you must walk in with your management team—those who will manage the project—and the management team orally presents its plan to the government. How do you turn that into a competitive advantage? This is a major change in the way business is done in a huge market. In the past the government might never have seen the management team. They might have met the project manager, but never the team. So now we are preparing managers to present themselves properly and professionally to the customer. That caused us, and every other company, to train managers in presentation skills, which we never had to do before. You have a competitive advantage when your team can very professionally present their plan. Companies that cannot get through an oral presentation today probably will not get that piece of business. We just train our people better. With the help of electronics, we also make sure we present a better proposal, with better graphics, a video tape or multi-media CD-ROM. These are ways to get a competitive advantage.

KEEPING ON TOP OF THE COMPETITION

Competition is different. Today because of technology we compete with start-up companies. In the past they wouldn't have had a chance. Just look at the information-technology services market today. Companies in business today that weren't here ten years ago are an absolute threat to AT&T. Consider what MCI has done.

The startups come up with creative ideas to compete. Look what Microsoft did—it gave products away free. That was a change that enabled it to leapfrog over its competitors. Who ever heard of giving your product away free? It caught the whole industry off guard. What do you do with a competitor that gives products away for free? It challenged everyone.

I preach constantly that everyone is a change manager. I emphasize that positive change doesn't mean reacting to external forces, it means creating change. I tell people that at some place, some competitor has a bunch of people figuring out how to beat us. They're going to do something different and better than we do—changes in the marketplace that will make it a stronger competitor. Then we'll have to react to that. When you start reacting to changes that are imposed on you, you're usually trying to catch up. If you do catch up, you're only even. Good competitors will constantly change the dynamics, culture, or circumstances of a market so they can be in control.

We try to be proactive, initiating change that will cause our competitors to react. In almost every instance where we offer a proposal to a customer, we try to be innovative, to offer something different from what a competitor may offer.

MANAGING EXPECTATIONS

Years ago, people would come in for an interview and they'd say how much is the pay... then of course, what are the benefits. Later candidates started asking what is the pay, benefits, and what's the work environment: Where will I work, how big an office will I have, will I have a window? Now it's about pay, benefits, work environment, educational benefits, continuing educational opportunities, and dress code. I'm serious. Certainly, the question is often raised, "Can I work at home—why do I have to come into the office?"

You accommodate them the best you can. Working from home is a good example. I read there are 22 million people working at home now. Think of the money that saves those companies. For starters, they save an average of 120 square feet of office space per person. Real estate people don't like that. But why should you have an employee come to the office if they don't have to be there to work. Today managers can say, "Here's the project, what we're trying to do, here's your role, just deliver your piece of the project. We don't care if you do it at home or from the back seat of your car." With that kind of work environment, leaders need a different attitude.

It presents a bit of a problem for leading. Not everyone can work at home. But for those who can, you have to be willing to consider that option. Some companies today do not have offices or paper. They communicate entirely by e-mail. I'm reading more and more about executives who say, "Do not send memos—use e-mail or I will not respond." Talk about change.

There is a potential negative to this because when you totally drain personal relationships out of an organization, it won't be as strong. There's something to be said for people seeing each other periodically—maybe not every day, but working together face to face. A $50 million company here, Microstrategy, is run by a 28-year-old. The company now has 450 employees, is now worth $473 million, and has gone public. The founder believes strongly in personal relationships. One of his trademarks is that he shuts the company down once a year to take the entire company and their families on a cruise. He wants to build teamwork and relationships. Some don't work at the same office, but he clearly is the type of leader who wants some type of personal relationship with employees. Not all leaders are that way.

Both systems work.

Many employees have expectations about their future that are not realistic—promotions or greater responsibility. If they aren't able to perform on the job, for whatever reason, they may have to be fired. I don't know anyone who doesn't have a hard time with that except the hard-hearted Hannas who would never be good leaders. I always say, "If it ever becomes easy to fire somebody, I'll go find another job."

People nowadays want to be on the cutting edge of technology. They want to be using the latest tools. Each time they hear of a new software package coming out, they want to use it. Everyone thinks they need the most powerful computer to do their job. They don't.

Lots of people today also don't want to be involved in the routine work. It's hard to get people involved with just maintaining systems.

Leaders need to deal with this on an individual basis. There's no formula.

Chapter 2

JAMES CHAMPY

LEADERSHIP SUMMARY

Currently Chairman of Perot Systems Consulting Practice and formerly Chairman and CEO of CSC Index, James Champy has overseen many breakthrough organizational change efforts. Champy is a leading authority on the management issues surrounding business reengineering, organizational change, and corporate renewal. As co-author of *The New York Times* best-selling book *Reengineering the Corporation* and author of *Reengineering*, also a bestseller, Champy clearly established himself as one of the founding fathers of the reengineering movement. A regular columnist in *Forbes*, *Computer World* and *Sales and Marketing Management*, he feels that, while times are changing, effective leadership requires certain basic capabilities, such as sensing ability and an ambition for the business itself, integration skills, and empathy. Among current leaders he respects are Jack Welch, Gary Wendt, George Hatsopoulos, Ken Lay, and Jim Rogers.

■ WHAT'S YOUR PERSONAL VISION OF A GOOD LEADER?

Times are changing, as you say. But it's the context of business that's changing, like major competition and technology. I feel there is a need for leadership to get back to basic principles. Business conditions are changing, but a lot of the questions about what to do are the same. There are some underlying elements of leadership that are reasserting themselves. One is the pure nature of ambition itself, in the good sense.

How do you mean that?

I mean that you must be ambitious for the business, not necessarily just ambitious for yourself. There are two tests I have always applied when I have gone to companies that say they want to change or want to do major re-engineering: First, what is the ambition of the management—the nature of their ambition, the extent of their ambition? Second, do they have an appetite for change? If the answer comes back positive to both of these, then I have always felt that the enterprise stood a chance of doing something great. If it wasn't there, then the change would only be incremental.

When you assess the appetite for change, there must be some kind of feedback you get, some signal that tells you the commitment is real and positive.

Yes. The signal that I look for is whether managers are willing to act on really hard issues. There are many companies today who haven't gone through a lot of the changes they will have to go through, operational and otherwise. These changes will be heavily focused on logistics and relationships with customers. There will be a lot more integration between customers' and suppliers' business processes. Reporters call me and ask "Isn't the age of re-engineering over?" I tell them I really believe it is just beginning. There are a lot of companies out there, and actually a lot of the nonprofits in particular, that have not yet gone through the degree of operating change they will ultimately have to go through.

■ WHAT ARE THE DEFINING CHARACTERISTICS OF A GOOD LEADER?

One is what I call a "sensing capability." It's an ability to really sense what's going on in a marketplace and determining what to do about it. Or being able to enter a whole new market or experience a whole new set of conditions and sense what's happening. The more a business is affected, particularly by information technology, the greater the need for that sensing capability; sensing when is it necessary to take action; when your business is dead or when it will die in its current form; being able to predict that.

Do you think a lot of that is inborn or can it actually be learned?

I think it takes a certain inborn sensing capability. The capability can be sharpened and developed but it's an intuitive thing. You can bring all kinds of analysis to the table. Take the simple example of the publishing industry.

If I came to you and said the future in publishing isn't in print anymore, it's in some other media, you might say 50 years from now that may be the case but not five years from now. And you are probably right. But the question is, What do you do about it now? When do you act? For example, when do you try to make money in an Internet kind of business that has never made money before for anybody? But yet you know somehow that the future is in some kind of electronic commerce. These are the kinds of very tough questions that require some sort of intuition. When do you start changing the fundamentals of your business model?

What else?

There is another capability that leadership requires today. Let me describe it as integration skills. It's how to work across functions and across business units within your business. How to fundamentally rethink the way integration happens within the company. And to continue to chip away and get rid of the inefficient fragmentation in business transactions. Longer term, it's how to make integration work across your company and your customers and your suppliers.

Is that another one of those either-you-have-it-or-you-don't type of skills?

I think there are pieces of leadership that are innate, that people are really born with, and there are other skills that are developed over time through the experiences that they have. There are those who will take experiences and develop and grow. I hold leadership as something that isn't easily taught. You are right in the sense that there are some people who will have certain experiences and who will not assimilate them. But there will be leaders who know how to take those same experiences and learn from them. The fundamental elements of leadership are innate, and then it is developed through a set of experiences and decisions you make over time.

There is a third element, empathy. It requires a person to have a deep feeling for, and respond to, the changes that people are going through, whether it's loss of their jobs or a change in their work. And your ability to lead an organization comes from the respect that people have for you, not from any power that your position gives you. It comes more from who you are. It's more existential than emanating from some position in the hierarchy of your company.

How do you develop this respect?

It comes from the substance you demonstrate; about what you know about the business, about the industry, about how to do things, about how to make things work. And, again, the word I am using is empathy, a real sense of caring as people go through major change.

A real life scenario: How do you get cooperation from people in a situation or a process where half of those sitting at the table won't be there in a year. This is not a made-up situation.

You are right. There are two approaches to that. The first is you make the decision sooner rather than later not to have those people sitting at the table. Or you demonstrate to them that even if they are not there, you will be truly humanistic in how they will be treated. You'll take as good care of them as you possibly can. Even then, you may not get everybody's cooperation. The hard reality is there are no guarantees that anybody will have a job, or the other way around, there is the truth that certain people will not have a job.

■ HOW DOES A LEADER GET PEOPLE TO FOLLOW?

So how do you pull the people rather than push them in business?

It really comes down to who you are and what you stand for. To get people to follow you they have to believe you truly know something about the business and about the industry you are in. People have to trust your business judgment. And secondly, they have to trust your values. And then they are likely to follow you. A piece of those values is around your empathy, your caring for people. The great leaders have both. They care for the troops and they understand how to fight the battle.

■ HOW DO YOU DRIVE LEADERSHIP DOWN INTO THE ORGANIZATION?

You have first to recognize that inspiration comes not from just the way you communicate as the leader but from the conversations that go on at every level in the organization. It's impossible for a single leader to drive down the message of change and inspire people at all levels. What it takes is a hierarchy, or a network, however you want to describe it, a set of people who are really in partnership and who are having conversations with everybody in the organization about the nature of change, what is driving it and what it means for people at all levels in the organization. It isn't until you are having those conversations deep in the enterprise that there can be any sense of inspired leadership. In the end, it has to come down to a personal level.

So people need to know what's in it for me?

That's right.

HOW DOES A LEADER DEVELOP A TEAM CULTURE IN AN ORGANIZATION?

You actually make it crystal clear what it is the organization means by "culture." You get very clear about the expressed values of the organization. Today there is almost an atmosphere of cynicism out there. I may go and say here are the five beliefs and values of the organization and initially there is a tendency to reject the beliefs. A team culture won't get formed until people see behaviors that demonstrate those beliefs. A second requirement for a team culture is that people have to like each other. Sometimes people are forced into situations where they don't get to choose who they work with. If you're lucky, they will like each other. If they don't, a team culture may never develop.

HOW DO YOU ATTRACT THE BEST PEOPLE – AND KEEP THEM?

Attracting good people is always a challenge for companies. If you want to attract the best people, not just the brightest but those who will have the right ambition, the right motivation, the right qualities, what attracts them is the opportunity to create something new. Many young people are going to high-paying big banking and financial services firms to do big deals. They may be doing big deals. But are they doing anything new? I don't think so. They are often driven by greed. Now there is some value in a little greed, but in the long run, companies that have people who are solely driven by greed will not create the best kind of enterprise. I think the people who are really the best people, who I would want to put in a boat setting out to sea on a new adventure, are smart people who would be excited about the opportunity to create something different and something new, something that meets a real need out there that nobody else has seen or discovered yet.

That would seem to explain a lot of the attraction in the technology field.

Yes. This is an extraordinary time because technology is giving us an opportunity to create a lot of new stuff both directly at the technology companies themselves and in all the industries that are affected by technology. There are also a lot of risks as only a few of these leading-edge companies will succeed. Sometimes, it's because people are ahead of the times. Sometimes it's because the ideas aren't very good and sometimes the ideas are very good but there isn't the management skill to succeed.

■ WHAT ARE THE MAIN CHALLENGES TODAY'S LEADERS FACE?

There are two different sets of challenges.

One is knowing when to act.

My advice is sooner rather than later. Technology compresses everything in time.

The other set of issues has to do with the rate in which you can expect to make organizational change happen. There are people who conclude that they have to change the way they do their business. And it has to happen fast. We still haven't invented processes that accelerate organizational and behavioral change. It's still a five-year process. So one of the major challenges is how to get change to happen more quickly.

Would that in part explain why a lot of change fails? If you're thinking something is going to happen in a year or two and it doesn't, that creates a major disconnect.

You can get some change to happen in a year to 18 months. But major change in most medium to large companies is still a five-year process.

How do you cope with the endless barrage of information flow?

There is a very simple answer to this complex problem. You have to choose who and what you listen to. Do not allow yourself to become overwhelmed. You have to create filters. I heard it said somewhere that the urgent forces out the important. You get information. You get signals. They all pretend to be urgent. All trying to get your attention and often succeeding. You have to exercise some judgment in who you listen to, whether it be some news-service or a group of managers. There is, of course, always a risk that in doing that you will cut off something that's important but that's part of your skill in being a manager, to sense what's important and worth listening to. The idea of being open to everyone and to everything is, I think, a naïve notion. But you don't insulate yourself. You have to venture outside your circle. Find wise people whose judgment you respect. They can be your co-workers, your customers, your suppliers. They should come from different places. But you have to identify who they are. Otherwise there is a good chance you'll listen to fools.

■ HOW DO YOU DEAL WITH BURNOUT ON A PERSONAL LEVEL AND AMONG THOSE ON WHOM YOU COUNT MOST AROUND YOU?

There are people who can do all kinds of wonderful things with their lives. But it's true in corporate America (even in Europe and in Asia) that it's becoming increasingly difficult to separate your personal and work life. The company wants more and more of your time. It will take all that you have to give. And personal life is becoming very difficult. You have to set the limits. And by the way, that's true for both the leader and the worker. As a leader you have to tell people and show people, set examples of how to set boundaries between work and other activities. Let them know about your activities. Send a signal that it's okay to draw the line. Now that doesn't mean you don't mix business and pleasure at times but you have to signal to the rest of the workplace that it's okay to take a vacation. I had a person in the "delivery room" whose wife was having a baby and he called me on the phone to talk about business. I simply said, "What are you doing calling me? Get off the phone!"

Don't you think some of that happens out of fear?

Sure, but that's why you have to set the tone. And say it's okay.

■ WHO AMONG LEADERS OR MANAGERS WOULD YOU CONSIDER TO BE A MODEL IN THE CURRENT FAST-CHANGING ENVIRONMENT?

The quintessential guy is Jack Welch. It's true. He has all those qualities, sensing capability, the right sense of where to integrate, what to do, and so forth. And he has much more of a humanistic sense than he is given credit for. I have experienced him personally as being very caring.

Anybody else?

Gary Wendt who works for Welch is another exceptional leader in a very different way. He leads with such power and substance and a command of what's going on that it's quite remarkable.

Is there anybody who isn't so much on people's radar screens yet who you'd care to mention?

A guy who is not a household name yet is George Hatsopoulos who runs ThermoElectron. A wonderful leader. He is a marvelous combination of ambition and intelligence and caring. He has developed a cadre of exceptional managers to run the company. He has great breadth.

Another guy who does get some press but is not so well known is Pat McGovern who runs the big publishing company IDG (International Data Group). They publish many of the information technology journals, *Computerworld* for example. He is a marvelous guy who has built a huge privately held company. He shares the ownership broadly with his people and gives them accountability and responsibility. He moves around guiding and helping and prompting his people. I like that. But he is not out there leading with just vision. He's very solid all around.

I also like a few other people. Ken Lay who runs Enron is very strong. And Jim Rogers. Both in the utility industry where leadership is very critical these days due to extreme market and supply conditions, as well as government deregulation.

■ WILL TOMORROW'S LEADERS BE ANY DIFFERENT FROM OUR STEREOTYPE OF TODAY'S TOP EXECUTIVES?

There are still many executives today who represent the remnants of the way the game used to be played: being groomed, and going through a series of jobs while being developed to take over the top position. But many of the true leaders of tomorrow will have a different ambition, of wanting to do something great for the business not just for themselves. That separates them from many of their predecessors.

Chapter 3

MORT FEINBERG

LEADERSHIP SUMMARY

Mortimer R. Feinberg, Ph.D., is chairman of the board and co-founder of BFS Psychological Associates, Inc. and Professor Emeritus at Baruch College at the City University of New York. He is a former industrial psychology consultant at Mt. Sinai Hospital, a lecturer and instructor at Columbia University Graduate School, and author of six books, including *Why Smart People Do Dumb Things* (with Jack Tarrant, Simon & Schuster, 1995). He has acquired a vast amount of knowledge about leadership, not least by having interviewed four U.S. presidents.

■ DO YOU HAVE A PERSONAL VISION OF GOOD LEADERSHIP IN THESE TIMES?

I think that the most important thing is: Know what you want to accomplish in your company. What is your vision for the company? I don't mean just a dreaming vision but a projection of the imprint you want to have at the end of your regime. What is the task you put in front of you? You have to think through very clearly what your business mission is, what you are getting paid to do.

Second, you have to know what basic resources you need to accomplish your mission: economic, people, the kinds of relationships you need with your people, your suppliers, and your customers. You can't just say, "I'm Moses. I'm going to lead you to the promised land." You have to say, "I need 30 horses and 20 mules." You need able people. As Jethro, Moses's father-in-law, said to him, "Moses, you're trying to do so much yourself. Go out and find able people. Some can lead ten, some can lead a hundred, some can lead a thousand." By the way, that's how the Mormon church organizes themselves—into leaders of tens, hundreds, and thousands. Let your people solve all the soft causes themselves, and bring only the hard causes to you for resolution. You should also talk to them, so they'll know the difference between a hard cause and a soft cause. What they can do themselves and what they need to bring to you. Eighty percent of the issues they can solve on their own. They should know what are the critical issues that need your time to resolve.

Next, create a boundaryless culture, as Jack Welch says, where people can work together toward a common good—to sacrifice their immediate egocentric needs toward a goal. The hardest part of leadership is to get people willingly to do what's necessary for the accomplishment of the goal, to submerge to some degree their own present, short-term needs, to accomplish the mission of the organization.

Third, a leader needs just plain, sheer physical energy. People are energized by energetic leaders. They do not respond well to an uncertain trumpet.

Finally, make certain that the message is heard throughout the organization. As the president of the Bank of America once told me, "When I give a bugle call, I think it's great. By the time it gets down to the teller, it's often perceived as a belch." So a good leader should be able to communicate his mission to the entire organization.

■ WHAT DO YOU SEE AS THE FIVE OR SO DEFINING CHARACTERISTICS OF GOOD LEADERS AND MANAGERS?

I'd list vision, equipment, energy, and a boundaryless culture, where you break down the turf and everybody works toward a common vision.

■ HOW DOES A LEADER GET PEOPLE TO FOLLOW?

By his energy, example, value system, and moral courage. That's one of the problems with Clinton right now. People doubt his moral commitments, his lying. You can't be caught in a situation where you're perceived as less than honest and candid, as manipulative. An example in the business world would be when somebody tells you they're going to do something with regard to the mission, and they don't follow through. Or they say, "This is our value system" or "This is our mission," and then go out and do something that contradicts this. For example, a company that says they're basically oriented toward consumer disposables, and then goes out and starts buying machines. That's one thing that successful presidents do.

Welch says, "I'm going to be first, second, or get out of the way. We're not going to be third or fourth in the market."

■ HOW DOES A LEADER INSPIRE LEADERSHIP AT EVERY LEVEL OF THE ORGANIZATION?

He's got to wander around, use all the vehicles possible, sample all levels of the organization. He's got to make everyone feel they're having fun working toward the mission, that the company celebrates accomplishments. Southwest Airlines does a lot of that. Their mission is to be much more oriented toward customer service. In one case, a flight attendant had a woman passenger who had diabetes. The flight was delayed. The stewardess took the woman home and called her husband and made certain she took her shots, then took her back to the airport the next day. This was celebrated throughout the organization—in the company newsletter, in a notice sent to all employees, flowers that were sent to her family—as an example of their mission. They did everything to ritualize the celebration. The employees are empowered this way.

■ HOW DOES A LEADER DEVELOP A TEAM CULTURE IN AN ORGANIZATION?

Remember: Teams are people with complementary skills committed to a common purpose. So a leader has to be able to set up teams that have a chance to work together frequently, have a clearly defined mission. He's got to be able to eliminate levels of command, so people feel they are the hierarchy, that there's a lot of lateral communication between the different groups. He leads through diversity, rather than conformity. These are some of the recommendations that work in terms of a common purpose.

■ HOW DO YOU ATTRACT THE BEST PEOPLE?

By your own example, by being the kind of organization that people want to work for. That becomes the attraction: a company that's willing to take risks, that promotes trust, interdependence, and hard work. You also attract people by exploiting the power of positive feedback, giving out gold stars, celebrating successes. These things are an essential part of the structure. When people are deciding where to work, their criteria are: Is it a successful company with a future and a mission? Is there growth opportunity? Remuneration is important, but it is a hygiene factor. Having the right economic incentives isn't enough.

■ WHAT ARE THE MAIN CHALLENGES TODAY'S LEADERS FACE?

Picking the right team, having the right mission, recognizing what your competition is, and encouraging self-assessment. Leaders have to ask, What is our mission? Who is our customer? What does the customer value? What is our plan? Also, they should do benchmarking; that is, they should compare their firm to competitors'. One of the best examples I know about is a company that was involved in the delivery of cement. They said to themselves, "Instead of benchmarking against other companies that deliver cement, what is the best fast-delivery company?" They came up with Domino's Pizza. They got the maps from Domino's—what roads they used, how they used them—and they were able to significantly decrease the time it took to deliver the cement.

■ HOW DOES A LEADER/MANAGER COPE WITH THE SEEMINGLY ENDLESS BARRAGE OF INFORMATION?

He's got to be able to sort out what's important, what he needs to address today and what can wait.

You've got to think like a doctor arriving at a battlefield, and decide which patient needs immediate attention and who can wait. The doctor can only depend on his own judgment. There's no substitute for judgment and knowledge.

■ HOW DO YOU DEAL WITH BURNOUT, ON A PERSONAL LEVEL AND AMONG THOSE ON WHOM YOU DEPEND THE MOST?

You've got to watch and make certain they get sufficient reinforcement. Burnout is the feeling of lack of accomplishment, that they can't get on top of their jobs. It's possible they're overloaded, their energy is wasted, they're not focused. There are also personal situations that interfere with capacity to work, so you have to be aware of what's going on in their lives.

■ WHO AMONG CURRENT LEADERS OR MANAGERS WOULD YOU CONSIDER TO BE MODELS IN THE CURRENT FAST-CHANGING ENVIRONMENT?

Cal Turner, Jr., at Dollar General. Danny Bottoff of First America. At the university level, a guy named Steve Sliwa, who runs Embry-Riddle Aeronautical University in Daytona, FL.

■ WILL TOMORROW'S LEADERS BE DIFFERENT FROM OUR STEREOTYPE OF TODAY'S TOP EXECUTIVES? IF SO, HOW?

Yes, in that they have to be much clearer in their vision and much more aware of global competition, which didn't used to be a problem.

Chapter 4

FRANCES HESSELBEIN

LEADERSHIP SUMMARY

In July 1976, she left the mountains of western Pennsylvania to become CEO of Girls Scouts of the U.S.A., the largest organization for girls and women in the world. She worked with the Girl Scouts for 15 years—about 5,000 days—and "I never had a bad day." She left the Girl Scouts in 1990, to become president and CEO of The Drucker Foundation, a nonprofit group that "leads social sector organizations toward excellence and performance."

■ DO YOU HAVE A PERSONAL VISION OF GOOD LEADERSHIP IN THESE TIMES?

Leadership is a matter of how to be, not how to do it. We spend our lives learning how to do it, but in the end, it's the "how to be" that defines the quality and character of our performance and contribution. A good leader embodies the vision, mission, and principles of the organization.

■ WHAT DO YOU SEE AS THE FIVE OR SO DEFINING CHARACTERISTICS OF GOOD LEADERS AND MANAGERS?

First, a leader is mission-focused. A leader leads by example and from the front, with clear, consistent messages and values that are moral and a sense of ethics that works full-time. Leaders acknowledge that people are their greatest asset. The really great leaders I know manage for a mission, innovation, and diversity. As they manage for the mission, they share a vision that they hold before the people. Their employees know why the leader does what he does.

■ HOW DOES A LEADER GET PEOPLE TO FOLLOW?

You gain their trust. Someone said, "Our country was built on the principle of leading with faith and following with trust." But I think you have to build trust and you lead by example and with language, by persuasion. You transcend the old barriers and definitions. In the beginning, the leader bans the hierarchy. We get rid of the old hierarchy that most of us inherited, and we develop the kind of flexible, fluid management system that really reflects the mission and vision of the organization. Once we have the kind of flexible, fluid structure that releases the spirit of our people, then we also look at the old "gospel"—the collection of procedures and assumptions that are part of the past. Peter Drucker has a wonderful term called "planned abandonment," and when we practice that, we abandon old policies that will have little relevance in the future. Then we try to use a new kind of language. We abandon the old "command-and-control" language of leadership. I would purge from the vocabulary the words "up" and "down" and "superior" and "subordinate" and "ladder," and adopt a new language of leadership, where we believe that our people are our greatest asset. Leading people, not containing people. You cannot talk about values and principles unless your behavior reflects those values. You have to recognize the power of language and use it to mobilize people around the mission of the organization.

We must also practice "disbursed leadership" (other people call it empowerment), where we don't have the *leader* or *a leader*, but leaders at every level of the organization.

■ HOW DOES A LEADER INSPIRE LEADERSHIP AT EVERY LEVEL OF THE ORGANIZATION?

Through example, language, and inclusion. Also, understanding that people are watching, and there's nothing more inspiring than having a leader's behavior match his language. Then we must practice appreciation and inclusion as we build tomorrow's organization and look at the customers we're serving now and the ones we want to be serving. A leader has really scanned the environment and identified the one or two trends that will most effect the organization, and explains the implications of those trends. We're not flying on assumption; we've examined the background of our planning. Then, we look at the organization; we look at the diversity, the inclusion of a richly diverse workforce, board, or staff.

One of the great questions for any organization is: When the customers look at us, can they find themselves?

We also manage for innovation, which I define as "change that creates a new dimension of performance." Change shouldn't be a threat but an opportunity, and we help our people to see that.

■ HOW DOES A LEADER DEVELOP A TEAM CULTURE IN AN ORGANIZATION?

By using all kinds of teams, having a very open working environment, and appreciating the team approach to management. And making sure each team has a task. There's a clear definition of responsibilities charged to the team and differentiation of roles and responsibilities. For instance, if it's a short-term team based on accomplishing a specific goal, this should be made clear. You can't develop a team culture; you develop the teams, and in the working of the teams, the culture is developed.

■ HOW DO YOU ATTRACT THE BEST PEOPLE?

This is a great challenge to the organization's viability and relevance. We attract the best people by creating an environment that encourages staff development, leadership, and learning. We take seriously employees' personal and professional growth. We look broadly, beyond the traditional recruitment pool and old networks.

When I was CEO of Girl Scouts, I had 800 national staff members, 335 CEOs around the country, and probably 6,000 more executives. I took very seriously the leadership opportunities for every person. You look at Service Master, which I think is one of the largest service organizations in the world—and these are service workers who clean houses and serve food in cafeterias and take care of termites—and Bill Pollard, its CEO, says that every employee is a person of great dignity and worth, and deserves leadership development opportunities. It's part of his philosophy. If you really believe that an organization is its people, then you invest in good people. Then you expect them to take responsibility for planning their own development. These are the people who stay, because they can stay and learn on the job. They don't have to go somewhere else.

■ WHAT ARE THE MAIN CHALLENGES TODAY'S LEADERS FACE?

The Swedish Red Cross asked me to address its board and staff, the business community in Stockholm, 60 other organizations, and the media, on this subject: How can we transform the organization so that it is viable and relevant in the future without losing its soul? I hear this everywhere from leaders in all three sectors around the world. They're very concerned about the future and whether their organization will remain relevant in a very tenuous future. What are we doing today to ensure our relevance? You can't wait until the future hits you. So many of the old answers don't fit these new questions. We must revisit our mission—and we recommend that people do this every three years—to make sure it's still a clear statement of their purpose. And if our environment or the needs of our customers change, we need to revise our purpose to make sure it's a short, compelling, passionate statement.

Another great challenge reflects what is happening in the world around us: Governments are relinquishing the social services they've traditionally provided. Businesses are unable to pick up what government is relinquishing and the nonprofit sector can't provide what government and business are unable to provide. So the great challenge is social responsibility. How do we meet the needs of children, families, and communities when there are such great changes? We believe that the day of partnership is upon us. The great challenge for corporations, government, and nonprofit organizations is to find a partner(s) and together address a critical need in the community. We find that some of the best-led, best-managed, most successful corporations are the ones that are practicing this. We are very passionate about moving beyond the walls to build a community with the same energy and commitment used to build the enterprises within the walls. More and more, in all three sectors, we're realizing that one sector can't do it. We think that's the bottom line for the million nonprofits in this country: changing lives and building community. Corporations looking beyond the walls understand that a sick, ailing community cannot provide a healthy, energetic, competitive workforce in the future. It's an exciting time because a lot of the global barriers are down.

■ HOW DOES A LEADER/MANAGER COPE WITH THE SEEMINGLY ENDLESS BARRAGE OF INFORMATION?

You manage it. We don't have to do everything. We have to decide: What is the information we really need to be effective? How do you identify the priorities for your leadership? What are the tools we really need to use? There are people who say, "I have a thousand e-mail messages." Well, do you really need a thousand messages?

■ HOW DO YOU DEAL WITH BURNOUT, ON A PERSONAL LEVEL AND AMONG THOSE ON WHOM YOU DEPEND THE MOST?

I've often found that what we call burnout is frustration. Leaders can become frustrated with their inability to move, can feel so contained and boxed-in that they don't have what they need to be effective. So the person to whom that person reports ought to be asking, "What can I do to be helpful?" How do we unleash our people? Give them the resources they need to achieve high performance.

■ WHO AMONG CURRENT LEADERS OR MANAGERS WOULD YOU CONSIDER TO BE MODELS IN THE CURRENT FAST-CHANGING ENVIRONMENT?

One of the most exciting and productive leaders is Louis Platt, CEO of Hewlett Packard. When we asked him to write about the organization of the future [for a Drucker Institute book], we expected him to write about cyberspace. But he said, "I would like to write about employee work-life balance." That's one of the greatest challenges of the decade. That's a real leader, because he really believes that an organization is people and they are its greatest asset. Everything I read about Jack Welsh at GE, especially his passion for education for his people, and the time he spends with his leaders and employees, impresses me. He said that ten years from now, when someone looked at the GE report card, he hoped they would see that the company cared as much about the hearts and souls of its employees as the bottom line. I think he has a real interest in the development of his people, and he invests heavily, not only with resources, but with himself. General Dennis Reimer of the United States Army does a superb job of leadership development at every level.

■ WHO AMONG CURRENT LEADERS OR MANAGERS WOULD YOU CONSIDER TO BE MODELS IN THE CURRENT FAST-CHANGING ENVIRONMENT?

In many leaders, we see a passionate focus on mission. Peter Senge, author of The *Fifth Discipline*, has said, "Mission instills the passion and the patience for the long journey." Just the bottom line will not be the focus of tomorrow's leading executives. I think they will transcend the old stereotypes of today. They'll build that richly diverse organization. They'll see the most important investment will be in their own people. Mission and vision will be a palpable part of their leadership.

Chapter 5

THOMAS R. HORTON

LEADERSHIP SUMMARY

Thomas R. Horton is a former senior executive of IBM and retired CEO of the American Management Association International. He has served on the boards of many companies, from start-ups to listed large-cap corporations, and as trustee of a number of colleges and universities as well as many non-profits. He is currently a director of the National Association of Corporate Directors and a columnist for *Directors & Boards*.

■ DO YOU HAVE A PERSONAL VISION OF GOOD LEADERSHIP IN THESE TIMES?

Leadership is a very individualistic thing; it has to do with a leader being fully himself or herself, and motivating others to be the same. There is no cookie-cutter or cookbook rule on leadership. It's a matter of getting the job done. Charisma can play a part in it, but it's not the essential thing. I've known some noncharismatic leaders who are very effective.

Who?

Abraham Lincoln was noncharismatic. He had a peculiar squeaky voice; he was hard to hear, had sort of an Ichabod Crane kind of an appearance, tall and thin, not an attractive man to look at.

What do you mean being fully oneself?

I think when I say being fully oneself, I mean drawing very deeply on one's well of knowledge and well of experience and convictions. And being authentic; a genuine person. When one does that, he or she is respected for it. That's not the reason to do it; the reason is a matter of conscience and self-respect, and also for the purpose of being able to draw on the energies and everything else one has when the best is needed.

An example?

Let's take an entrepreneurial setting. We are leaders of our organization and we're going to mold our organization into whatever it is. It's going to mirror our values and our beliefs. Can you do the same thing with the same effectiveness when the organization is very large? Yes, you can; that is, provided the organization's culture in which you're imbedded is compatible. If it's your own company, it will be. It flows down from you, at the top. But the company culture could be affected by the founder, or it might not be your company and the culture there is incompatible with you. Then you can't be that effective. And this leaves you with choices: adopt the values of others, which I think is a mistake, or go somewhere else.

■ WHAT DO YOU SEE AS DEFINING CHARACTERISTICS OF GOOD LEADERS AND MANAGERS?

INTEGRITY

The absolute basic building block is integrity. A lot of leaders don't have it. It's not a matter of degree. Either you have it or you don't. There is someone cutting a corner here or shading the truth there, and I get very nervous. It's not a matter of degrees. You have to have an absolute commitment to it.

A part of one's commitment to integrity is truth. And truth is reality. By this I mean not allowing one to fool oneself. Having that reality is the bedrock of everything. It's easy to get disconnected from reality the higher one is, and you have to constantly look out for it.

Of course, quite apart from the moral issues is the practical issue: Without a real grasp on reality, the solutions you've come up with to solve this problem or that will not work.

COMMUNICATION

There's a kind of communication that involves the sharing of one's perception. If you're the chief executive officer or general manager of your division, you have many more opportunities to see what's happening around you; your view is from a higher vantage point than those lower down in your organization. So if you want me, your employee, to be fully effective, you have to share these perceptions.

It's teaching, but it's also a spirit of generosity; a willingness and an eagerness to share the insights you gain from the opportunities you have. You have to have an eagerness to do it, to help people develop themselves, to become fully themselves, which goes back to my initial vision of leadership.

ALERTNESS TO OPPORTUNITY

Rosabeth Moss Kanter, a sociologist who is teaching now at Harvard, wrote *Change Masters*. She is a very astute observer, like Peter Drucker, whose greatest value to my mind is his ability to observe and analyze and describe what he sees. Anyway, she devoted a paragraph or two to the concept of luck. Almost all successful people you talk to, somewhere in the first couple of sentences, will say, "I was in the right place at the right time." She says you also have to be the right person; otherwise you might have just overlooked the moment. What I mean is, you also have to be opportunistic, you have to have an awareness of opportunity. I mean this in a positive way, the ability to take advantage of opportunity, being alert to opportunity. Louis Pasteur said luck comes to those who are prepared. I think the French translation is "Chance comes to the prepared man."

You hear that someone is always one step ahead, that they can see around the corner. I don't think great people can see around the corner; they just can see further. You have two fishermen fishing beside each other on the dock. The first fisherman has a net that's six feet in diameter. The second fisherman has a net that's twelve feet in diameter. They're fishing in the same water with the same amount of fish. The fisherman with the twelve-foot net is likely to be luckier.

The same is true for the person who has the opportunity to get around more, visit more places, meet more people, meet people at different levels, get to know more kinds of customers, get to know more vendors. The person with these opportunities, all else being equal, will be luckier.

This is another reason that you want to help your people be fully themselves, to experience more. I'm very lucky in that I know enormous numbers of people. Of course, I'm 70 years old. But a good part of this is that I remember them. I keep track of them—where they are now, what they're doing.

DECISION MAKING

When does a decision need to be made:
This is very important to understand. It is sometimes very difficult not to make a decision. You have all the data in front of you, you're very aggressive, a type A personality, and you want to make a decision and get it behind you and go on. But if you make a decision too early you're missing information. You want to make it when it needs to be made.

Here's an obvious example. Let's say you're going to decide how many silk purses you're going to make two weeks from now. You don't need to make the decision yet. You don't know how many customers you'll have. But you decide to make this many and go to two shifts. By god that's what is going to be done. Why? Because you have the authority and power to do it.

The reality is there are more people who know more about it than you do, and they should be the ones making the decision.

You can't afford not to delegate and to trust those under you. I have a big decision. I need to figure out who is this decision going to affect besides myself. It's those most strongly affected; they're the ones who should make the decision. And that does require trust. That is also where the matter of earnest communication needs to take place. Give me whatever input you can.

It gets down, first, to the question, Is it time to make that decision? I'm trying to be nondecisive so that when I make that decision it will be better. Second, Am I the person to make the decision and, if not, who is?

A third element involves identification of the consequences of that decision—what actually did happen. Should we have waited? Could we have had better data? You have to analyze your mistakes in decision making. It's seldom the case that you make a right or a wrong decision. More often the case is, If you do it this or that way it's more probable that this or that will happen. You are choosing between a set of probabilities that one thing will happen over another. The third outcome is the unforeseen consequence, the unexpected side effect.

It's not what you expected but it may have elements in it you can make use of. You need to be alert to what comes out of unexpected consequences.

In the end, if you can't do the right thing, make it right. This was the attitude of the former IBM CEOT. Vincent Learson. His philosophy was, If the ceiling is falling in, what can we do to shore it up?

FOCUS

The ability to focus, to absolutely focus—this is where many potential leaders fall short; they don't focus. You look at Jack Welch of GE, one of the world's best listeners, although he doesn't suffer fools gladly. He's an added value kind of manager and he's bright enough that he can focus on this or that particular problem while bombs are going off in other parts of the company. Not many people have this ability. It requires sheer intelligence, true—there's no substitution for that. But I know many who have the intelligence but lack this focus. It's intellectual muscle, not just brainpower. A matter of discipline. It's the mental equivalent of the guy who can do 112 situps. Thomas J. Watson Sr., founding CEO of IBM, said, "If you want to think well, just think hard."

Is it innate or can it be learned?

It can be learned.

Many people think they cannot grasp something. You just have to ask them some questions. It's a matter of going to someone who does have the concept and spending enough time with them to get it. If you have a minimum of intelligence, it goes back to fully mentally exercising your brain.

TENACITY

Focus has to do with subject matter; tenacity is sort of the little rat terrier with his teeth around your foot...the tenacity of that dog; he has no concept of why he's doing it, he's just going to stick with it.

You stick with it, no matter what?

You don't if you have some clue you're going the wrong way.

It's a rare quality but a common quality of great leaders. Ronald Reagan had a few of these simplistic beliefs that he talked about and stuck to and everyone understood that was what he was about and that's why people admired him. His successor, George Bush, went from one damn thing to the other. And we're not too sure what Clinton's up to.

■ HOW DOES A LEADER GET PEOPLE TO FOLLOW?

LISTEN

You have to genuinely listen to other people, and have a genuine interest in them. Any time I've gone into a new job, I spend a month going around, being a detective, turning over rocks, asking people what rocks need to be turned over. I say, "I don't know a damn thing about this place, you do. Tell me what you think I should know. I need your help."

And if they come forward and tell you, stick their necks out and complain?

You must maintain confidences absolutely, to deserve their trust. Don't do something you said you're not going to do. Don't not do something you said you would do. If you make the mistake of committing to do something you thought you could do but can't, go back and apologize and explain, or you will lose trust. Once trust is broken it's hard to repair at any level.

Something else about listening: Consider genius. No one has a monopoly on great ideas. Anybody could be on their way to work and have a stroke of genius. If I'm a good leader, I need to listen to the guy out in the car pool who has had this idea. If I don't listen, he may tell my competitor. The leader has a dual role: to communicate in broad strokes where we're going, and to listen to all ideas coming from all quarters. Ideas come bubbling up, some good, some bad.

DEMONSTRATE COMMITMENT

Demonstrate your own commitment. Say you're a captain in the army, the infantry, and you have a 24-mile hike the next day. You can go in the truck or you can march with the troops. If you want to be followed, you better march with the troops. Sure, later on, maybe you can ride in a truck—you're a captain after all—but you earn the ride in the truck.

GIVE DIRECTION

You've got to give some clue as to where you're going. Without it, they'll follow you for a while. But then they are going to say, "Hey chief, where are we going? What about new products? What about new markets?" They're not going to follow if there's no place to follow you to.

In any organization we all have to be clear as to what our purpose is, our mission, down through the ranks. Everybody has to share this—the secretaries, the people in the shop, the people in the field maintaining the trucks. For two reasons: One, for cohesiveness. Two, for spiritual reasons. If I know that a whole community of people share the same mission or goals, then I feel as if I belong to a group, a group that shares a common purpose.

The purpose is not to make money. It might be to provide the lowest cost banking in the United States or the highest level of service in lodging in a four-star hotel. If I'm the U.S. Mint, then my purpose is to produce money, or if I'm a counterfeiter, at least to make something that looks like money. Otherwise my purpose has to be something that relates to the customer. Finding some way to distinguish me from my competitors and relate to customers. And it has to be something I can get behind. Can I commit my life to making shoes? I don't know. Can I do so for cigarettes? I've smoked them most of my life (though not now) but no...Having a purpose is how we know why we're here.

■ HOW DOES A LEADER INSPIRE LEADERSHIP AT EVERY LEVEL OF THE ORGANIZATION?

(Dr. Horton answered this in part when he talked about what is required to get people to follow, and earlier when he discussed the importance of communication and a generosity of spirit that shows itself in a willingness to trust others and to share perceptions. He elaborates here.):

You can talk about people skills, interpersonal relations—they're absolutely important. There's also conformity to the industry you're in. Some people can be a CEO in two or three industries. Some people are only good in one place—the right place for them. But essentially it's a matter of finding the right people around me whom I can tolerate and who can tolerate men like me. It's better for us to be different. We are going to be fully ourselves, we're going to keep each other as informed as possible, share insights so that we can leverage our intelligence, make the best decisions, focus on what we're trying to do. With this combination, we're going to succeed.

■ HOW DOES A LEADER CREATE A TEAM CULTURE IN THE ORGANIZATION?

One way is to make sure that everybody knows that problems and opportunities don't have single owners. So, for example, take the most difficult kind of organization, a functional one. You're the CEO and you have someone in charge of manufacturing, someone in charge of engineering, of marketing and so on. We all know that there are marketing problems that have nothing to do with manufacturing, but you treat it like a well-kept secret. So what you do is you get them to meet together, put them in a room, don't give them any food and a limited amount of water and leave them in there until they decide they're running out of water and will do almost anything to get out of there. In other words, pretty soon they'll catch on that the issue is what do we do about this challenge or opportunity, that it's ours to solve. Very often someone without a marketing background comes up with the solution to the marketing problem, and someone not in manufacturing comes up with the solution to the manufacturing problem. It's a matter of reaching outside our "box."

Another part of this is expectation: making it clear to your people that you are looking for a team, not a gang of individuals. This means they have to take risks, but it also means you have to take risks, have to be willing to roll up your sleeves and get involved in the process. Not everybody is suited to it, to team play. I knew an Italian executive, the late Marisa Bellisario, in charge of the communications corporation Italtel Societa\Italiana Telecomunicazioni. She said to me once that she noticed she was a great team player so long as she was captain of the team. Some people are loners, wonderful at individual tasks. They'll never be a good team player. So don't buy a cow to win a horse race.

■ HOW DO YOU ATTRACT THE BEST PEOPLE?

That's a tough one. The first thing is, you have to have the ability to identify them. This is the most difficult of all. It often requires help.

Headhunters?

The opinions of other people around you. Once I had a problem with a chief financial officer; I didn't know enough about the financial side. I needed people to sit in on the interview. But, of course, the interview is the least of it. Much more important is someone's track record. People have to have done something, have made something happen. They can't just have been around when something happened.

Assuming you can identify them, how do you get them?

You've got to have a challenge, something that's exciting enough for people to want to get involved in. You can't recruit great people for a humdrum job. There's got to be a challenge, but yet hope of success.

You also have to give people a really long leash. This is the most important thing to many people. Praise is good, but the best praise is saying, "Charlie, you handle this problem. You let me know when I can help you." Charlie and I need to have some agreement on the kinds of decisions he can make without letting me know and what kinds of decisions I have to know about.

One way to test this, to evaluate someone, is when you're on vacation you turn over responsibility to the person whose judgment you're trying to evaluate. You tell them, "I don't want to be bothered by a lot of phone calls but I also don't want a mess when I get back; you can call me but don't call me very much." It's a great way to test people.

■ WHAT ARE THE MAIN CHALLENGES/ISSUES TODAY'S LEADERS FACE?

If I were running a *FORTUNE* 100 or a *FORTUNE* 10 company, when I get to the office in the morning, some of our most urgent problems would be on the front page of *THE NEW YORK TIMES*. They would have to do with the human condition. When Carter was in office, one question would have been how many people the U.S. had in Iran. Now it might be trade in China. Top leaders are always facing major and unexpected crises as well as intractable problems from below, some that perhaps have no solution.

More specifically?

FAIRNESS

Leaders constantly face the issue of fairness. There's a story of a former CEO at DuPont years ago. He's presenting to his board his strategic plan to increase market share of some chemical. Everyone is enthusiastic and ready to applaud. Then one director says to him, "Yes, but is this fair?"

Fair to whom?

To competition, to our employees, to suppliers . . . What is fair to the shareholder is not necessarily fair to others. Leaders are constantly looking for balance in all of these things.

PEOPLE DEVELOPMENT

For the people in the organization, I have to provide proactive opportunities for them to develop themselves. For example, if I'm the chairman of Proctor & Gamble, there's never enough people of top talent. I want the most talented people to know I love them, I believe in them. Pragmatically, this is what you call preventive maintenance. Keeping them around.

To groom people for top positions?

You can say to them, "I don't know if you'll advance but lets work toward that probability. You tell me what you think we need to do to heighten that probability and I'll tell you what I think and we'll work on it together." It takes a lot of trust.

COMPLIANCE

Compliance with regulations and laws, as well as our own regulations. Deciding how compliant we want to be on government regulations. Do we want to be barely compliant or to get ahead voluntarily? These all have to do with our values.

EXPANDING BUSINESS

Creating new customers and new markets.

■ HOW DOES A LEADER/MANAGER COPE WITH THE SEEMINGLY ENDLESS BARRAGE OF INFORMATION FLOW?

Eugene Fubini, former deputy director of defense, used to say, "If you want a sip of water you don't take it out of a fire hose. But if that's the only source, you step aside when you do to drink from it. You sample it at its edges."

It's the same with information. Say I don't know much about some field of information. I would need a person to act as interpreter of the data. Another way to look at it is to ask yourself: "If I were on a desert island for a year and could only have four numeric indicators of how my business is doing, what would they be?" You probably don't want earnings—that won't tell you what you need to know to run the company—but maybe you'd want the volume of business, market share, and a couple of other things. You don't need all the stuff you get. You might almost say to yourself, "What would a member of the board of directors need?" I can always find out later how many tons of size eight shoes we shipped to East Wichita, but I don't need that right now.

■ HOW DO YOU AVOID BURNOUT PERSONALLY AND FOR THOSE AROUND YOU?

That's a good question and I'm not sure I have the answer because I've had several burnouts. Once I was on a terrible two year assignment that involved 14-hour days, going into the office on Saturday mornings. I went in one Sunday morning and there was someone waiting there to see me and I thought, "This isn't working." I thought a lot about quitting. It was in a poorly organized part of the company. I had almost no clout. I had to do it all by persuasion. It was a terrible but absolutely central job. I felt like I was hammering down a piece of plywood and every time I got to the fourth corner the other three would pop up.

I decided I was going to leave and figure it out later. My wife and I went to Nassau with a return ticket but no reservation. For three or four days I just lay in the sun, not even trying to read. I was gone about 10 days altogether, and when I came back, things at the office were better. People had stepped in in my absence. I had a lot of support, they knew I was burnt out. Of course, I was the one who was screwing up but I didn't know it. When you're burnt out you make the wrong decisions.

I went to see the CEO, Tom Watson Jr. Actually he asked me to see him—he heard I was about to leave. He did reorganize, and gave me another job. It was also a terrible job, but I coped, because I knew I could just get on an airplane—that I wasn't indispensable. Nobody is."

Do you advise sending someone who works for you off for a week like that?

Yes I do. The best thing to say to someone is, "The problem will still be here when you get back or it will be worse. Either way we can work on it then. If you call me when you're on vacation I'll be furious." I've done this with people and it's worked.

The real answer is to avoid it happening. John Opel, chairman and CEO of IBM for two or three years, was a really able guy. He used to go home on time. He was a bird watcher, a "birder" as he put it, and he loved opera. He had a wonderful physique. He was in his 60s and he looked 35. He had superb self-confidence. When he took over the CEOship of IBM he said to me, "I'll work eight hours a day. That's all I'm going to give them and ....if they can't take a joke." It takes a strong attitude not to get sucked into the maelstrom.

■ WHO AMONG LEADERS OR MANAGERS WOULD YOU CONSIDER TO BE A MODEL FOR TODAY'S CURRENT FAST-CHANGING ENVIRONMENT?

Besides the ones mentioned above, Father Theodore Hesburgh, retired president of Notre Dame, and the current CEO of Alcoa, Paul O'Neill.

Hesburgh was such a human being. He had an enormous capacity to listen, and he had integrit; he was, after all, a priest...The same is true of O'Neill. Now, aluminum is a tough industry, a commodity, very price sensitive, it's one globally competitive business. O'Neill arrived at Alcoa and after a couple of days he was asked what he was going to stress. And he answered, "Safety." His reasoning was if we had safe plants we would have control of the manufacturing process, cleanliness, quality, and a better price, all of which would drop to the bottom line. "You should expect whatever you inspect," according to the late Larry Appley, former president of the American Management Association. O'Neill would go into every meeting, and instead of asking what revenues were that week, he would ask about safety and quality. He understood consistency and focus. This takes enormous self-confidence and guts.

■ WILL THE FACE OF LEADERS TOMORROW BE DIFFERENT FROM OUR STEREOTYPE OF TODAY'S TOP EXECUTIVES?

What I would wish, and I don't know if it's possible, is for a little less reverence, a little more irreverence, the ability to put themselves in perspective, to see that their job is not saving the world. I meet a lot of young people, I meet students every day because I hang out a lot at Stetson University, and I see younger managers and younger CEOs than when I was starting out, and I think they do have a better ability to let the water run off their backs.

How can they believe they can afford to do so in today's competitive environment?

They have to! Otherwise it will drip on their heads.

Chapter 6

VICTOR KIAM

LEADERSHIP SUMMARY

Victor Kiam is an entrepreneur and currently is chairman of a wide range of consumer, industrial and high-tech companies, including Remington Products LLC, Ronson Inc., Citadel Technology, Inc., the Francis Company, Lady Remington, and Pic Design. His management philosophy is "Lead by example, try to instill an entrepreneurial spirit throughout the organization not based solely on monetary rewards, and be constantly alert to the changing global and domestic marketplaces and the effects of peripheral factors on the business."

■ DO YOU HAVE A PERSONAL VISION OF GOOD LEADERSHIP IN THESE TIMES?

A good leader must, after reviewing all the factors, be decisive. In certain areas where the leader has expertise, he should take the initiative and provide an example to other members of the organization about the nature of direct involvement.

■ WHAT DO YOU SEE AS THE FIVE OR SO DEFINING CHARACTERISTICS OF GOOD LEADERS AND MANAGERS TODAY?

First, he's got to be honest and fair. Second, he must be able to have an equanimity in all situations that shows the other members of the organization that he has a steady hand on the tiller (he should not wax ebulliently and be effervescent in good times, nor should he be moroseful in poor times). He should have a high energy level. He should be familiar not only with the immediate competitive situation facing the business, outside factors that could impact the future of the company but that other members of the organization might not foresee. He should maintain a strong organization of entrepreneurial people who are cost-conscious and financially astute.

■ HOW DOES A LEADER GET PEOPLE TO FOLLOW?

By example, not only by his daily work habits but his good decisions. If he has all the other qualities—honesty, fairness, etc.—but over a period of years he has six major decisions and blows them all, some of the members of the organization might highly suspect his ability.

■ HOW DOES A LEADER INSPIRE LEADERSHIP AT EVERY LEVEL OF THE ORGANIZATION?

When I got into Remington, the morale was horrible. We had a debt-equity ratio of 50-1, and everybody wondered whether we'd be around the next day. I instituted a lot of things, but the one that had the greatest effect on all the people was that once a month, I gathered the whole company—the finance area, the marketing people, everybody—onto the factory floor, where the manufacturing and assembly workers were—and they were paid on a time basis but we'd shut down and absorb the cost, every month for 15-20 minutes—and I told them exactly how the business was, what were the positives and negatives I saw for the past month, and what it looked like for the future. So they felt like they were part of the business, and they felt that if they worked a little harder, maybe they could change the fortunes of the company. Of course, during this period, I was convinced that we could be a success. I didn't get up and say, "In 30 days, if we don't do this, we'll be out of business."

■ HOW DOES A LEADER DEVELOP A TEAM CULTURE IN AN ORGANIZATION?

That can be done on several bases. Instead of having a one-on-one interface with the senior executive with that team, when the team is formed, you clearly identify that this is a team effort. When there are meetings between the key leader—

the executive who set up the team—and whoever is making out the report, a substantial number of people on the team are present so they feel they're getting an equal opportunity to have an interface in the direction that the team is going.

■ HOW DO YOU ATTRACT THE BEST PEOPLE?

By creating an environment that makes the work process as enjoyable as possible, in conjunction with the hard work that has to go on. You do it by offering them an opportunity to prove there's a meaningful basis for their optimism—that they can grow within the company. Setting entrepreneurial reward standards; for example, individual bonuses, team bonuses, corporate bonuses for performance. In general, if at all possible, promote from within. Lastly, make sure that the standards established throughout the company, which might emanate from the personnel department, the finance department, etc., are fair and people can see they're justified. Don't be arbitrary and don't let your predilections sway what are considered good business practices. For example, personally I don't mind flying tourist except to the Far East. So I made a corporate resolution that everybody flies tourist except to the Far East. It was pointed out to me that I might be injuring individuals or hindering some people's ability to perform work during transit time. You see, there are a lot of people who have difficulty flying tourist because of age or physical problems or like to work during business flights. So for these people flying tourist might be a disadvantage going to or returning from Europe. So I made exceptions.

■ WHAT ARE THE MAIN CHALLENGES TODAY'S LEADERS FACE?

Boy, there are so many. It's a much faster global economy. Things that used to take years to evolve now happen in two or three months. You have to be able to move quickly. Indecision can be a trap that can kill you. You must be decisive after you've gathered all the facts. On the other side of the coin, there are so many other opportunities, especially in places you never considered before. It's a constant review of the position and direction of the company. Most companies have a monthly review, and there is a list of priorities that is prepared based on that review. Progress on those priorities is measured at the next meeting. What's amazing is how many new priorities crop up each month. That's the major change I've noticed, and I've been at it for 47 years. There are other areas of change, too. The way it used to be, people in every area of business didn't have the information they do now to make decisions. This has changed the whole methodology of the interface between various components. In the old days, salesmen could go in and give a highfalutin' projection and a song-and-dance and probably get a good order for a promotion based on hype. Today, the more advanced retailers of the world—not just here, although we're more advanced than most—will look at their sales rate by stockkeeping unit, what the trend is, the current inventory situation, material situation, margin, and make a more rational decision than they did in the past.

In the past, it was more of an emotional decision. So the differences are accelerated pace and globalization and greater information available on every level.

■ HOW DOES A LEADER/MANAGER COPE WITH THE SEEMINGLY ENDLESS BARRAGE OF INFORMATION?

You've got to know what information you shouldn't get. If you give a list of reports to a project manager or factory superintendent, generally speaking they'll check off everything, because they feel if they don't do it, somehow or other, they're not considered to be really involved. After awhile, you realize that they never look at half of the reports. So one of the things you have to know is the information that people use. One of the ways you can do that is to constantly revise the numbers and the variation of the types of reports that people get. That means you have to have a full review every six months to make sure that people are reading the reports they get, not just throwing them in the wastebasket. There could be too much information. If you're involved in a business, part of your responsibility—and this isn't just for the chief executive, but goes down throughout the organization—is to read the trade journals relative to the manufacturing equipment that you use, to be aware of any changes so you can replace the machine or upgrade, to get lower costs. From a marketing point of view, you have to read the various publications and trade reports relative to the products, services, or industry you're involved with.

■ HOW DO YOU DEAL WITH BURNOUT ON A PERSONAL LEVEL AND AMONG THOSE ON WHOM YOU DEPEND THE MOST?

I have never really burned out myself. I'm an optimist; I like life, and I always look forward to turning over the page to see what's ahead. I'm always curious and enthusiastic, and obviously driven to have a success. If you can instill that or have people around you who are the same way, you're not going to have burnout.

There are two cases I remember: In the '50s, we had a chap who was a very well-qualified guy whose brother was in the same organization. The first guy was transferred to Germany. About a year later, I had a call that something strange was happening in Germany, that there were strange vibes coming from there. I had nothing to do with the German operation at the time, and because the president of the company thought nobody in Germany would be threatened by my presence there, he asked me to go there. I was supposed to say I was making a worldwide appraisal of businesses we're in around the world, and looking for other lines. In that guise I might be able to find out what was going wrong there. Well, once I got there, it didn't take me too long to find out what was wrong. The guy who we'd sent over was the only American in the company, among indigenous Germans. Somehow or other, he'd gotten the feeling that the German people were out to get him, and every night, he packed up his entire office and took it home with him. All his papers. It would take him an hour and a half to pack up every night, and an hour and a half to unpack every morning. He'd gotten such a persecution complex that he would write in an illegible manner. I asked him, "Why are you writing like that? You can't read it." He said, "Nobody else can, either." When I came back, I said, "We got a problem." We flew the guy back and he was institutionalized.

The second example was more recent. He'd been in business for over 35 years, and with one of my companies for over 25, with hardly any time off. I hadn't seen him in about six months when I went to visit him. He'd gotten very heavy and I noticed he was very lethargic—, he moved slowly. I took him out to dinner and we had a lovely chat and he began to wax philosophically and I said, "You put on a lot of weight. What's happening?" He replied, "I don't know. I think I'm going through male menopause. I think I'm trying to rationalize what my life is. I've never married, I've been working and too busy, and I don't get the excitement that I used to get going into the office." After a few more days with him, I told him to take a leave of absence.

So a manager should be sensitive to the people around him. I've found in going through the corporate world, there are one or two executives with whom I'd built a relationship that transcended nine to five. On several occasions, I've gone to them and said, "I've got this problem. What do you think?" They had nothing to do with business. And I had dinner overseas about a month ago with a friend who manages a major investment fund. We were walking back to the hotel afterward and talking and he asked me how long I was married and I told him over forty years. And he asked, "How did you manage that? You travel so bloody much and you're always away." And I told him you've got to be sensitive; that when I am home, I spend as much time as possible with my wife. And he said, "I hadn't really thought about it that way. I try to spend time with my children but I take them alone, without my wife." I said, "You're leaving her out of the equation," and he said he would definitely include her in the future. Those are the kinds of human interfaces that can be very beneficial if your advice is good.

■ WHO AMONG CURRENT LEADERS OR MANAGERS WOULD YOU CONSIDER TO BE MODELS IN THE CURRENT FAST-CHANGING ENVIRONMENT?

Margaret Thatcher. I think the decisions she made to change what had been a drifting society, to get it focused on the future and to redirect it, were just amazing. It was an extraordinarily painful process, but the United Kingdom has emerged as one of the economically successful countries. Without her vision and ability to get support to do what she did, it wouldn't have happened.

    In the American corporate world—and I'm only going to talk about people I know personally—there's Andrall (Andy) Pearson, who was chairman of Pepsi Cola, became a tenured professor at the Harvard Business School, a partner in a leveraged buyout firm (and chairman of several companies they bought out), and now he's chairman of the board of Tricon. He had a successful career in every one of his endeavors and is a renaissance man in many ways. He only took over Tricon a year ago and their fortunes are already reversed. And then there are men for their own time; for example, Lee Iaccocca's rebound of Chrysler, when he came in and completely changed direction. Another chap who has a lot of the qualities I mentioned earlier is Thomas Murphy of ABC, with whom I worked over 40 years ago.

■ WILL TOMORROW'S LEADERS BE DIFFERENT FROM OUR STEREOTYPE OF TODAY'S TOP EXECUTIVES? IF SO, HOW?

The chief executive of a large global company must have a credible group of people that can analyze all the factors going into the global environment, and must look beyond the day-to-day business at least six months out. You've got to be constantly aware of what might happen. People who are running a business day-to-day without a defined group of people who are evaluating the future will be subject to wrenching events that they can't anticipate.

Chapter 7

ED RIDOLFI

LEADERSHIP SUMMARY

Ed Ridolfi, vice president of executive development for the McGraw-Hill Companies, supports the visionary mode of leadership. He believes that truly great leaders are visionaries and mavericks who dance to their own drummer. They are high-energy people filled with enthusiasm, while being down-to-earth enough to bring their visions to fruition. Mainly, they know how to motivate others and delegate.

■ DO YOU HAVE A PERSONAL VISION OF LEADERSHIP?

I view leadership as different from managing. I make that distinction because leadership is really about getting ordinary people to do extraordinary things. Leaders are people who take you to places you've never been before. Managers get things done. They implement strategy. Managing is about blocking and tackling. Leadership is about defining strategy.

One is not more glamorous than the other or better than the other. What I am saying is that there are times and events that occur in business that require those specific competencies. For instance, when a business is doing very, very well, the tendency is to lay back and ride the tide. The reality is that you need to be looking beyond where you are, at the next thing you ought to be doing.

A leader is the one who can see beyond the current circumstance to where the organization ought to be going, even if it's entirely different from where it is now. They catch the next wave, the next opportunity. Businesses need both types: managers and leaders. My experience is that it's rare to find great managers who are great leaders or visa versa.

Leadership is not magic. And it's not about creativity, alone. Leaders are very creative. They create solutions and see the possibilities, not the "what are's." They create the future by visualizing it now, at this moment! I don't think there's any magic about any of this. It all involves basic fundamentals. Management is about basics. Managers focus on making the donuts. Leadership is also about basics, but with a different set of rules. Leaders don't get bogged down with minutiae. They focus on the big picture. They're constantly asking questions. What is the strategic direction? Where do we want to be? What are the changes that are required? Where are we most vulnerable? Where are the opportunities? They can put all the pieces together and come up with a focus and a strategy to get there.

Leaders are people with a keen sense of what's going on around them. Some folks question whether leaders are born or made. That's not an issue. Everyone has that "stuff" in them. It's a question of whether that stuff can be developed. I once heard a successful leader talk about how he became a leader. It all boiled down to early childhood development. He was of the opinion that if we didn't do the leadership, take-control things at six or nine-years-old, it didn't mean we couldn't succeed. We just have to run faster and work harder at being a successful leader.

It's not like leaders are born with creativity. You certainly can teach creativity; teach people to unleash the creativity within themselves. What leaders have that's different is an innate sense of managing time to their best advantage. They do the most productive thing, every minute of every day!

What's missing today is time to be contemplative; time to think, to contemplate the business environment. Today, people are bombarded with information. They're caught up in the day-to-day. They don't take time to think about the broader issues. Their focus is too narrow.

■ WHAT DO YOU SEE AS DEFINING CHARACTERISTICS OF GOOD LEADERSHIP?

What distinguishes a successful leader? I have a short list of leadership competencies because I don't think it's very complex. There are some leadership competencies that are more important than others. Some of the elements I mention below are competencies that managers must demonstrate on a regular and consistent basis. Then there are others that belong to the bigger picture. Those are leadership elements for the rare individuals who are able to get the pieces together, get the bigger picture, and have a clear concept in their head of where they should go and why.

First, leaders have a high level of integrity. They uphold certain standards of quality and ethics every day without exception. To me that means demonstrating integrity in the way they deal with people, customers, colleagues and others. "Don't do as I say, but as I do" is not integrity. You don't lie once in awhile. Leaders have very high standards of ethical behavior and live them, day-to-day. They take full responsibility for their actions. Integrity is the central ingredient of successful/effective leadership.

Besides integrity, here are some other leadership competencies (see bulleted items; the other points are core competencies, not basic elements of leadership):

• Focus on results. Whether you "drive for it" or "focus on it," leaders make results their highest priority. It's the end game. It's their highest priority.

• Motivating others. Leaders have the ability to get people to stretch; to reach goals beyond their limits. Leaders motivate by action, and by their enthusiasm and passion for what they're doing. Followers are motivated by rewards and recognition. That's different. Leaders think beyond the day-to-day with a longer-term perspective. They make following them an adventure. Managers usually don't do that. They should, but they don't. That's hard for many Style is certainly important. There are great leaders who can muster people to go down the wrong direction. That's why they have to have drive and focus. Basically, leaders get people to go on an adventure. There's a lot of charisma and simpatico between what people want as participants and what they can get. "Why did you sign on to that difficult assignment?" "It sounded exciting." " Why did you give up a good-paying job while your kids are in school?" "Because it was more rewarding work."

Someone once said that leaders are like "people who are chased by an angry crowd and who make it look like they're leading a parade."

• Strategic vision or thinking. Leaders must have a strategic vision, be able to think outside the box, and have a clear sense of where they and the organization are going. They have to understand what creates competitive advantage for their business and are able to translate that into the initiatives and priorities on the work level. They also need to understand limitations of their organization; of their people; of themselves. And they help their people factor in those limitations and capabilities when making strategic decisions.

• Communication. Communication is getting the thoughts in your head into the heads of others so that each has the same, exact understanding.

These communications must be transmitted in a persuasive and motivated message. Those are supporting leadership competencies.

• Customer/market orientation. A leader has to have a clear, overt customer and market orientation. This applies to external and internal customers, as well. The real success of a leader in an organization depends on his or her ability to anticipate and meet customer and market needs and trends. Trends are what make leaders "see" possibilities.

• Finding and developing talent. Successful leaders are excellent at attracting and surrounding themselves with talented people. They can recognize talent even though that talent may not fit the perceived norm. They're not looking at the trees. They're looking beyond that. They're seeing a talented person, not someone who dresses or talks differently. Leaders are smart enough to know how to surround themselves with talented people, get out of their way and let them do extraordinary things. The leader gets in the way if he overmanages. Most managers like to control things, be in charge. They talk about empowerment, but it's about them being in charge and you doing the work. Most are comfortable with that model. The reality is that in any situation someone has to be in charge. Leaders know they can delegate to others and still get to where their vision directs that they be.

• Accountability. I believe you can delegate responsibility and authority, but you can't delegate accountability. Accountability fits everywhere. Accountability for your own actions, accountability for finding and managing talent, strategies for customers and markets and the money you invest. Other leadership competencies like diversity and interpersonal skills, have a universal perspective. They're what I call "supporting" competencies.

• Enthusiasm and energy. Leaders are high-energy people. You can't have an intense drive for results and a burning desire to find and develop talent in others if you don't have high energy. Enthusiasm and energy are contagious. Infectious. Everyone around a successful leader becomes highly enthusiastic. A high-energy leader also becomes further energized by other high-energy people. They all attract each other.

Leaders must live these competencies to be effective. Everyone in the organization—leader, manager, associate—has to play the same tune to produce a symphony. If I had to focus on which are the key leadership competencies that define a great leader, I would focus on these. Others do matter, but there are always the priority.

(Mr. Ridolfi considers the issues of sexual harassment, diversity, safety, etc. to be business issues.) Manager and leader are each responsible for making sure their people have a friendly, safe, hostile-free work environment. I'm not sure these are leadership issues except that the leader must demonstrate their importance by his or her own actions. Leaders unquestionably must "walk the talk" on these issues.

Leaders see a trend, couple it with something more than intuition — piecing a, b, c, d —their own gut feelings, and observations and get this "Aha! experience." I think that's what is really going on! Observers say, "Where the hell did that idea/strategy come from?" Leaders see a mosaic.

Leaders are intuitive. They are able to develop a broad spectrum of their world. How? They read alot of different materials and subjects. They open their minds to possibilities; think outside the box in the extreme!. They even play with kids. Kids are very creative thinkers.

One of the differences between the stereotype manager of the 1970s and '80s and the manager of the next millenium is that the next generation of managers must be more like leaders. But it's so hard to focus on the big picture when you're being beaten up every day. Everyone needs to think about trends that expand their business. People say, "You're crazy." Who'd ever think of putting a coffee shop in a book store? Who'd ever think you could put a few chapters of a book on the Internet and people would give their credit card number and buy the book?

Who are these people who come up with these ideas? They work in corporations that are innovative and adaptable, where people are involved and empowered decision-makers, In a top-down organization, you have to get on someone's calendar to discuss an idea. In entrepreneurial companies, accessibility, nimbleness, and creativity are key. They are forward-thinking, unconventional, successful. We all need to find ways within our little parts of the world to replicate this entrepreneurial atmosphere.

■ WHAT ISSUES DO LEADERS FACE?

SELF-DEVELOPMENT

I believe strongly that all development is self-development. Everyone has a responsibility for their own development. A leader takes this responsibility seriously as part of a drive for results. The organization has a responsibility to provide a learning environment. But training isn't enough. Training isn't development. Development is a long-term process that requires lots of commitment, resources and time, and it's worth every cent. Training is only part of the equation. For example, I need a broader perspective on doing business in China—I have to know what are the skills to do that. I can get training on how to do that effectively. But that's not development.

Development is a series of activities, experiences, opportunities and events that are presented to people to maximize their own gain. This takes place over the long haul. How can training lead to development? If sent on an overseas work assignment, integrate yourself into their culture and environment. I learn their language, and send your kids to local schools. That's development! Did you learn something from that. You bet. Did it add to the sum total of your knowledge and experience? You bet it did! That's development.

Functionally, I believe a leader's job is to create an environment where learning and real development occur. It's the associate's responsibility to take advantage of that environment and integrate training into their own development.

SHARING (POWER, RESPONSIBILITY AND AUTHORITY, KNOWLEDGE)
Sharing is a real issue for some managers. They have to deal with it while leaders have to address it. Business is changing from a top-down, hierarchical model to a flatter, more collegial one that is also being driven by a huge social upheaval. Today's workforce won't tolerate others "telling" them what to do and keep their mouth shut. They want to share in the knowledge gathering and have an impact on decisions.

I believe these are all issues that today's managers are facing. The old managerial model focused on retaining control; being in charge. The new model involves being a coach and facilitation, empowering people, building relationships, and a heavy dose of sharing. Some managers see this as a conflict, but it's a conflict that exists only in their heads. The sharing mindset is one that managers will have to adapt to. Sharing is a competency that leaders quickly recognize and maximize on a one-on-one basis.

TECHNOLOGY AND THE INFORMATION EXPLOSION/GLOBALIZATION OF MARKETS AND CUSTOMER BASES
These are major sea changes that leaders must understand now and rapidly integrate into decisions.

DECISIONS
There's more information available today than any one person can gather and review, particularly as it relates to the decision-making process. Decisions will be made based on more information and at greater speeds.

With greater speed comes greater risk. No one can be certain about the success of a decision, but leaders are accustomed to that. Managers are going to have to wrestle with this change in decision-making. Managers are going to have to learn to cull, sort and edit information at greater speeds. Like newspaper editors, managers have to learn when they have a kernel of something relevant; store the rest and toss what's irrelevant.

There are millions of books and articles written on leadership. A true leader will grasp what is important from this literature and then put their own spin on what it means to lead in this new global economy. They will explore new markets that never existed five years ago, and reach out to them even if most of us can't grasp the impact they will have yet.

Leaders see opportunities because they're looking at information and trends; they sniff the air if you will.

UNCERTAINTY

The new global leaders will combine awareness of technology and a concern for creating a new global order that's more considerate than those of the past. One of the real leadership competencies of a global leader is the ability to effectively manage complexity and uncertainty. That's what being a global leader is all about! Global leaders move out of their orderly, familiar culture, and become comfortable with chaos. They reserve judgment and embrace others with different and often unconventional ideas and opinions. This is where communication skills come into play, as well as awareness of others.

MOTIVATION TO LEAD

I believe what keeps leaders motivated to lead is found in a quote from Shakespeare: "The chase is oft more valued than the catch." It's the game, the interaction, the challenge, the excitement and uncertainty. It's all about making a difference It's why some "do" and others "don't."

It's more than ego?

I'd say it's more than ego. It's self-confidence. Leaders have the conviction of their decisions. They're also smart enough to know they don't have all the answers and they need to listen. They surround themselves with competent people. People get excited being with and part of a mission, and so they flock to work with a dynamic leader. It's really very simple.

Chapter 8

GLEN TOBE

LEADERSHIP SUMMARY

Glen Tobe is the leader of the Change Navigation Practice for the Americas within Andersen Consulting and works with high-tech organizations, among others, seeking to manage and maintain market leadership in these turbulent times. He is the author of two books *Rekindling Commitment* and *Mission, Vision and Values*, and has been a faculty member at San Francisco University. Tobe works out of Andersen Consulting's San Francisco office.

■ DO YOU HAVE A PERSONAL VISION OF GOOD LEADERSHIP IN THESE TIMES?

There are several elements. You have first to break down the real and the aspirational.

The first element is authenticity or realness. Leaders need to communicate who they are as people. On the real side it's about: I'm a human being, I'm worthy of your trust, I make mistakes. The problem comes in when the aspirations side gets mixed up with the real. This gap is why no one can be president today. Everyone has a dark side, the stuff no one wants to know about. But we don't cut anyone any slack. We don't accept that gap between real and aspirational.

Everyone stands equal on earth, but the leadership position is by definition elevated, which means the light that gets cast on you casts a longer shadow.

A result of this is that leaders often find themselves lonely and ineffective. Part of this comes from what Robert Greenleaf, in his book

Servant Leadership, says is the Greek "primus." There is the traditional American work chart in which you have the vice president, etc—the tier below the CEO—answering individually to the CEO (picture a row of rectangles with lines angling up to the CEO box at the top). All directly report to the individual at the top, but the individual is isolated from the direct reports.

The alternative model is one of connectivity, where the leader is connected to the group. This is a big deal in effective leadership. Instead of a row of separate rectangles you have them merged into one long rectangle with the leader a small raised bump in the middle. In other words the leader has become part of the team.

It's a hallmark of these times of sound-bite madness that we have grown so intolerant of the frailty of our leaders. Everyone ought to look in the mirror before they start throwing rocks. The way leaders get around this is to know their own dark side. This is not a matter of preparation but of integration.

On the preparation side, the way you prepare others for it is to come into your position of leadership with humility, with a learning mindset, and create an environment of feedback and learning. You start by saying, "I don't know as much as you guys do, but I need to build a place here where we have candor and good will."

I start meetings with this. I am always meeting with people with tons more expertise than I have. I will never have the technical experience they do. But I do know how to get them mobilized. I get there early, turn on the lights and start the coffee. Then it's a matter of connecting with them.

Most people have issues with authority. There are two ways they deal with it: Suck up and go brain dead or reject it and throw rocks. The third way, and this a great leader brings to his company, is connectivity, getting people to be part of it.

Other issues:

A great leader today challenges the status quo; he or she is someone who can support the goals of a project through a real belief in people.

A great leader drives results. You have to have a keen eye. Keeping your eye on the target is really important. The challenge of leaders is to drive results while building an environment in which the team can be successful. There is an ongoing tension between your realness, your business goals, the demands of your role, the demands of the team. All those weave together. It's very complex.

■ WHAT DO YOU SEE AS THE FIVE OR SO DEFINING CHARACTERISTICS OF GOOD LEADERS AND MANAGERS?

1. The ability to build a collectively owned vision of the future.

2. The ability to build an environment in which discomfort and candor are key ingredients. By this I mean that the uncomfortable issues have to be dealt with. I'm not going to let people become brain dead. There obviously has to be an element of trust so that people will be willing to hear me. But as part of that trust I have to tell people things that are difficult to hear. Otherwise I simply become nice. Trust is implicit to a leader's success, but if the environment is such that discomfort is not part of the tension—you won't be talking about tough performance issues.

3. The heart of leadership is the recognition that you have to take care of your people. It's a complicated skill set. The most basic level is just to ask them: What do you need? On a deeper level it's building relationships with people in which they feel comfortable telling the truth.

The leader has to ante up first. You have to be the first to make the confession, to speak honestly. The good ones have a way of holding themselves—I call it presence—in such a way that they create an environment of honesty.

4. Learning. Someone I worked for asked me the other day, "How am I doing?" The degree to which the leader models the ability to learn and take and receive feedback is profound in terms of his or her ability to drive loyalty and business results. In the case of the boss that asked me this, I will go to the wall for her.

Take the opposite of this: With authority comes privilege and with privilege comes non-negotiable discussions which may be based on blindspots. An example comes to mind of a CEO I worked with who could not see why he shouldn't bring his daughter to a gathering to which none of the employees was to bring their children. I told him, "You're sending the wrong message," and he answered, "What do you mean?"

With authority come blindspots with more impact.

5. In *The Leadership Challenge* Jim Kouzas and Barry Posner talk about a variable that is a big deal to me. It is "celebrating the heart." There is always an emotional component to work. A leader unleashes the human capacity of people. A leader makes it more than just a job.

6. The ability to build adult-to-adult relationships at all levels of the organization. Hierarchies at their worst make people revert to being children. At their best, they become places where good ideas are shared and people with great experience mine the full capability of the group so that great ideas are generated. A garbage man can be a source of many good ideas. The classic example is what happened at Florida Power and Light. They were heavily involved in a quality effort, recognizing contributions of employees. They were giving out awards for anyone who improved quality and they gave one to a lineman who had figured out a way to minimize lightning strikes in Florida. As he received the award he said to the audience, "For thirty years you rented my hands; you could have had my mind for free."

7. The ability to take no action. I am continually humbled by the chaos that I have seen caused for others by well-intended action.

■ HOW DOES A LEADER GET PEOPLE TO FOLLOW?

What comes to mind are the qualities of being present and having presence. Having presence comes about when you've done some personal work on yourself; you've learned from your circuitous route to power; you've been fired, say, from jobs; you've worked out your demons, a bad marriage maybe, your relationship with your parents. The information you've derived from all this gives you understanding and presence.

The second part is staying present in the room. You may not know where you're going, sometimes you just don't know. Don't worry. Listen to what people are saying. This concept of leadership has built into it a notion of manipulation, that you can psyche them out. Don't try to psyche them out. You can't think it through without them. Think it through with them.

Take Sherlock Holmes and Colombo as models for leadership. Holmes is the great scientist, but he ponders the origin of a fiber, say, in the isolation of his library away from the scene, whereas Colombo determines the truth with the perp in the room. He is the better model for a great leader.

Another aspect to getting people to follow is that the great leader takes care of the environment of the group, he keeps them focused. He might not have had a clear pathway—a lot of time you don't—but he has faith that the group will figure it out. You don't solve the problem as an adult would for children. You look at what's happening to people around the room.

I was once involved in a key consultation to a company on a merger. I knew the CEO's position, that he was for it. The vote of his executive team was split evenly, 4-4. He could have voted and made it 5-4, but what he did was abstain. Instead of casting the winning vote, he forced the group to go through the thinking process again because he knew they were going to have to implement the decision. He took the opposing view in the discussion and argued eloquently against his own position.

When they voted again, it was 5-3 and he added his vote to make it a much stronger 6-3.

■ HOW DOES A LEADER INSPIRE LEADERSHIP AT EVERY LEVEL OF THE ORGANIZATION?

We live in an era where people have concepts of microwaving trust, turbocharging it. I don't buy it. You build relationships. When employees feel safe, when they feel cared for, when they feel heard, their trust tends to develop. When you're strangers to each other, if you don't know them, if they're objects to you, there will be no trust. When you talk about leadership cascading to all levels, I have doubts: I believe you can only have impact on the area with which you interface.

There are organization theories of how to build trust, but there are few examples. It's like world peace. It's a great concept but show me even the inklings. Businesses are not organized as experimental social labs. They are not tea groups. They're companies and there's always a balance between topline and bottomline indicators. You have to be cognizant that you're operating in a business environment. But you have to be part of it. You have to be down on the floor. A good example is a telecommunications company that had never had an order for more than 50,000 units a day and suddenly had to fill an order of 230,000. The plant manager shut everything down for a few minutes and went out onto the floor and asked, "How do we get this done?" The people on the floor had the answers and they came within a thousand or two of filling the order and would have made it had he not wasted time at the start huddling with the leadership team.

■ HOW DOES A LEADER DEVELOP A TEAM CULTURE IN AN ORGANIZATION?

It comes with the environment that the leader builds, the behaviors you model, and your ability to connect with people.

■ HOW DO YOU ATTRACT THE BEST PEOPLE?

That's a really tough one. The question of year 2000 will be, "Why work for anyone if I can work at home and be virtual?" The questions that have to be answered are: "What am I going to learn? What does this have to do with my calling?" By calling I mean there's a job, there's a career, and there's a calling. The question is: "Where am I going with this?"

A person's commitment to something—or in this case a willingness to commit themselves to an organization—has to do with a sense of belonging. It is intrinsic to the nature of society. The need to have a community is an implicit human need. The question here is: Belong to what? Another thing to keep in mind is that people belong to relationships rather than an organization. Organizations can provide a niche but it's generally temporary. There are times when someone may want to run their own company, times when they want to be part of a company. But the point is that these times change; we go through passages and rhythms. The idea of lifetime employment is no longer real.

If you're an A performer, you're 30 percent out the door as it is. If you're a star you know you're a star. To keep the A employee, or attract one, you need to give them opportunity, room for advancement, independence, freedom, and a challenging role. Then money is like sugar, alluring and sweet, but not nourishing and sustaining. You have to find them the roles they need, the roles that challenge them, to get them to come or to stay.

■ WHAT ARE THE MAIN CHALLENGES/ISSUES TODAY'S LEADERS FACE?

1. Technology. Technology is changing everything. A major change as regards the workplace is that technology is enabling people to work at home and people are starting to like it.

2. Women in the workforce. How to work it out well: how to deal with the problems faced by women who still have young children in day care or school; how to deal with the challenge of getting moms back into the workplace.

3. Until the last three months, the economy has been booming. There is a high demand for knowledge workers. This means the employee is in the leverage position.

4. People seeing more and more self-employment and outsourcing, the use of contractors. You can't keep people at the firm if they can go off and get several hundred dollars an hour as a consultant.

5. The challenge of building goal-based human-connected relationships. The human-connected part is so hard. If you want them to be just a resource, a body, a job, you're going to get mediocre performance, or someone vulnerable to the next headhunter who comes along.

There are predisposing skill sets that help you develop this. But I have seen so many different leadership styles, such a wide variety, from the serene, effective, totally at-peace kind of leader to the high-strung, neurotic type. And common to great leaders at both ends of the spectrum is that the people who work for them feel like they are under the leader's wing.

6. Figuring out what the leader needs to do to keep people cooking, feeling accepted, feeling heard, feeling safe, feeling they can tell the truth. How does a leader create an environment of trust? Socrates' three elements of friendship were knowledge, goodwill, and candor. I would say knowledge and candor are the elements essential here.

■ HOW DOES A MANAGER COPE WITH THE SEEMINGLY ENDLESS BARRAGE OF INFORMATION FLOW?

I face this all the time. It's a challenge for us all. There are two key things to deciding how to handle any given piece of information: One, who is it coming from, or which information stream is it coming from? Two, your internal sense of priority. If you're going to be successful in any company, you have to build a screen that prioritizes items: from the simple FYI item to information that has impact on people or your client or on your goal path. I have to know, first, what is the priority in the "breadth" framework and, second, what is the quality of my attentiveness—or "depth"—in that framework.

For the process to work you have to understand your own needs and those to whom you're talking in terms of communication. How you communicate, the form it takes. I want voice mail in one situation. If you have a 60-page work plan, I want that electronically. You have to set up a set of expectations as part of a system to govern what comes in.

You also have to use a chain of command so that your 22-year-old analyst works an issue before it goes to his 30-year-old manager, and so on up the hierarchy before it gets to me. I don't want someone circumventing the links in this chain and bringing me something before I should be seeing it. This means, of course, you have to delegate a ton of stuff. Leverage and delegate. You have to develop a certain degree of confidence that you don't have to know everything that you can stand on the shoulders of the experts.

■ HOW DO YOU DEAL WITH BURNOUT ON A PERSONAL LEVEL AND AMONG THOSE ON WHOM YOU COUNT THE MOST?

You have to build a calendar. You need to look ahead and see that you have some intensity here, a lag time there, intensity here, followed by lag time, and so on. You have to pace yourself—and those around you—as if you're running a marathon. There are no all-out sprints.

If you're going to bring creativity to your job, you've got to take care of yourself. Take care of your body, your self, your family. I travel a lot. When I'm home I go to see the neighbors and drink a few beers. I might play basketball. I do things that replenish me. I can't do these things every night but when I can, I do. Otherwise you get locked into an either/or paradigm. The paradigm is: I do exciting work and have no home life and have a money-generating shell of a life; or I have a boring job and am home all the time. The question is: How do I get the "and"? Life can not be compartmentalized except in the ideal—you have to weave the elements. When you are home, keep your mind fresh, see friends, don't think about work. Live in the "and." How does one switch the work switch off? It's called maturity and judgment. There's also the question of who do you become. What if you work like a dog for 11 months with the promise of taking the month of April off? Well, if for 11 months you're practicing being a dog, you become a dog, just a gentler dog for one month a year.

■ WHO AMONG LEADERS OR MANAGERS WOULD YOU CONSIDER TO BE A MODEL IN THE CURRENT FAST-CHANGING ENVIRONMENT?

Jack Welch—we were just talking about burnout. He rips people up who don't take time off. He continually brings a critical focus on what is a priority—in business as well as in terms of balance of lifestyle.

But I would say the best model would be Joe Costello, the former CEO of Cadence Design. He had a remarkable ability to learn. He would take one or two precepts I had given him and in 15 minutes not only extrapolate the essence of the issue or problem but run with it as far as the field had ever gone—to the edge of the envelope. It was not just a matter of his having a cunning mind, but he had a great touch for listening. He could really dig in and listen. It was powerful. His listening helped build his environment. His willingness to learn gave the people around him the courage to ask questions, because he would ask questions. He'd asked, What are the three reasons you believe that? But it would be asked with acceptance.

Of course he could pull down the hammer of accountability too.

He was the modern emergent leader. His goal was to make his company a great place to work, a great place to work with, a great place to be a shareholder in. He had a willingness to take risks. He was a true visionary with a lot of the core skills. He challenged the crap out of people.

■ WILL TOMORROW'S LEADERS BE DIFFERENT FROM OUR STEREOTYPE OF TODAY'S TOP EXECUTIVES?

They are going to have to be people who can deal with more areas of complexity, more information, and who have the maturity of judgment to screen out the real issues, to separate the wheat from the chaff. The game is more global so we are going to have to be more thoughtful. But technology will never replace relationships in the creation of comfort, acceptance, and a sense of belonging.

Leaders will have to be more human in this technology-dominated world. They will have to have the ability to get people to talk so that ideas come rumbling forward, to feel they are an integral part of something to which they belong—that they are accepted, that their contributions are noted; otherwise, the people working for them will become more isolated and separated and will stay connected to the organization only until the next headhunter comes along.

About the Author

Anthony S.Vlamis has over 25 years of experience in the business and professional and technical and reference publishing fields. He has been an executive and senior editor at Simon & Schuster, Prentice-Hall, AMACOM Books, and Van Nostrand Reinhold. He was a founder of Alexander Publishing & Marketing, a newsletter publisher and direct marketing services agency. As a packager and literary agent, he has customized information products for clients in commerce, industry and association environments. He resides in Rivervale, New Jersey and can be reached at intellagent@worldnet.att.net.

OTHER MANAGEMENT BRIEFINGS OF INTEREST

The Computer Time Bomb: How to Keep the Century Date Change from Killing Your Organization—Outlines the steps you—as a manager—can and must take today to correct this Y2K problem. Includes corporate profiles, case studies, and a 15-point self-test to see whether your organization is prepared to deal with this problem. Stock #2365XACZ, $24.95/22.45 AMA Members.

A Better Place to Work: A New Sense of Motivation Leading to Higher Productivity—Demonstrates that given the right working environment, employees can increase their productivity dramatically. You'll learn how to get employees to be involved, energized, more productive and to take ownership. Includes case studies and the latest research on motivation. Stock # 2363XACZ, $17.95/$16.15 AMA Members.

Beyond Customer Satisfaction to Customer Loyalty: The Key to Greater Profitability —Identifies the four stages of a company's evolution toward building customer loyalty and summarizes the key management principles that must guide the transition. Stock # 2362XACZ, $19.95/$17.95 AMA Members.

The New OSHA: A Blueprint for Effective Training and Written Programs— Explains the new law and tells which statutes are most often the subject of investigations and which require training. Models, step-by-step procedures, and additional resources are also included. Stock # 2360XACZ, $24.95/$22.45 AMA Members.

The Management Compass: Steering the Corporation Using Hoshin Planning— Examines the fundamentals of *hoshin planning*, a strategic management methodology which originated in Japan, that is gaining rapid acceptance with U.S. companies. Stock # 2358XACZ, $19.95/$17.95 AMA Members.

Mentoring: Helping Employees Reach Their Full Potential—Shows how mentoring has progressed to an information-age model of helping people learn, offering a wealth of management opportunities for organizational rejuvenation, competitive adaptation, and employee development. Stock # 2357XACZ, $14.95/$13.45 AMA Members.

Complete the **ORDER FORM** on the following page. For faster service, **CALL** , **FAX** , or **E-MAIL** your order.

Visit our web site: www.amanet.org

AMERICAN MANAGEMENT ASSOCIATION
INTERNATIONAL

MANAGEMENT BRIEFING ORDER FORM
(A multiple-copy discount is available. Call for details.)

Please send me the following:

☐ ____ copies of **Recharge Your Team—Keep Them Going and Going...**, Stock # 2366XACZ, $12.95/$11.65 AMA Members.

☐ ____ copies of **The Computer Time Bomb: How to Keep the Century Date Change from Killing Your Organization**, Stock # 2365XACZ, $24.95/$22.45 AMA Members.

☐ ____ copies of **A Better Place to Work: A New Sense of Motivation Leading to Higher Productivity**, Stock # 2363XACZ, $17.95/$16.15 AMA Members.

☐ ____ copies of **Beyond Customer Satisfaction to Customer Loyalty: The Key to Greater Profitability**, Stock # 2362XACZ, $19.95/$17.95 AMA Members.

☐ ____ copies of **The New OSHA: A Blueprint for Effective Training and Written Programs**, Stock # 2360XACZ, $24.95/$22.45 AMA Members.

☐ ____ copies of **The Management Compass: Steering the Corporation Using Hoshin Planning**, Stock # 2358XACZ, $19.95/$17.95 AMA Members.

☐ ____ copies of **Mentoring: Helping Employees Reach Their Full Potential**, Stock # 2357XACZ, $14.95/$13.45 AMA Members.

Name: _____

Title: _____

Organization: _____

Street Address: _____

City, State, Zip: _____

Phone: ( ) _____ Fax: ( ) _____

Applicable sales tax and shipping & handling will be added.

☐ Charge my credit card   ☐ Bill me   ☐ AMA Member

Card # _____ Exp. Date _____

Signature: _____

Purchase Order #: _____

AMA NO-RISK GUARANTEE: If for any reason you are not satisfied, we will credit the purchase price toward another product or refund your money. **No hassles. No loopholes. Just excellent service. That is what AMA is all about.**

Management Briefings
AMA Publication Services
P.O. Box 319
Saranac Lake, NY 12983
Visit our web site: www.amanet.org